HEALTH, PHYSICAL EDUCATION, RECREATION AND DANCE
MONOGRAPH NUMBER ONE

Healthy Moves
For Older Adults

Leslie A. Stenger
and
Christel M. Smith

Published by

CLEARINGHOUSE
ON TEACHER
EDUCATION

American Association of Colleges for Teacher Education
One Dupont Circle, Suite 610, Washington, D.C.
20036

February, 1985

CITE AS:
Stenger, Leslie A. and Smith, Christel M. (1985). *Healthy Moves for Older Adults* (Health, Physical Education, Recreation and Dance Monograph No. One). Washington, D.C.: ERIC Clearinghouse on Teacher Education.

MANUSCRIPTS:
The ERIC Clearinghouse on Teacher Education invites individuals to submit proposals for writing monographs for the Health, Physical Education, Recreation and Dance Monograph Series. Proposals must include:

1. a detailed manuscript proposal of not more than five pages
2. a 75-word summary to be used by reviewers for the initial screening and rating of each proposal
3. a vita
4. a writing sample

ORDERS:
The price for a single copy, including fourth class postage and handling, is $8.50. For first class postage, add $.70 for each copy ordered. Orders must be prepaid.

Library of Congress Catalogue Card No.: 85-070457

ISBN 0-89333-034-5

ERIC CLEARINGHOUSE ON TEACHER EDUCATION
American Association of Colleges for Teacher Education
One Dupont Circle, NW, Suite 610
Washington, D.C. 20036
(202) 293-2450

Series Editor: Laurie Priest, Associate for HPRD, ERIC Clearinghouse on Teacher Education. Ms. Priest also serves as Assistant Professor of Physical Education and Director of Athletics at Marymount College of Virginia.

This publication was prepared with funding from the National Institute of Education, U.S. Department of Education, under Contract No. 400-83-0022. The opinions expressed in this report do not necessarily reflect the positions or policies of NIE or DOE.

Contents

iii

Acknowledgements

The authors would like to thank several people for their support and assistance:

To Helen "Susie" Knierim for her suggestions and input;

To Helen Heitman, Jean Snodgrass, and Liane Summerfield for their comments and input as manuscript reviewers;

To Sarah Psitos and Devon Griffith-Phillips for their editorial assistance;

To Trish Sheehan and Mary Dangelo for their assistance in preparation of the bibliography; and,

To Laurie Priest and Celia Finstad, at CTE, who helped in various aspects of the review and editing phases of the project.

Preface

The "graying of America" is not a myth, it is a reality. As people approach older adulthood, it is important that they be encouraged to continue to live rich and full lives. Research has shown that a healthy, active lifestyle can enhance well-being in all stages of life.

This monograph is written to assist those professionals currently working with older adults and those students in health, physical education, recreation and dance professional preparation programs planning to work with older adults. The monograph addresses the older adult from not just a physical standpoint, but also describes some of the psychological and sociological aspects of aging. The authors' major focus is to identify the needs of older adults and outline the role of the health, physical education, recreation and dance professional in meeting these needs. The uniqueness of this publication is that it looks at the related fields of health, physical education, recreation, and dance and offers direction to the total profession for encouraging and providing healthy, active lifestyles for older adults.

Healthy Moves for Older Adults will show each of us that our profession can have a positive impact on the quality of life, throughout life.

—P. Stanley Brassie, Ph.D.
Chair, Health, Physical Education,
Recreation and Dance Advisory Board
for the ERIC Clearinghouse on
Teacher Education and
Head, Physical Education Department,
University of Georgia, Athens, Georgia

Introduction

Wellness programs are a vital component of our society for all age groups. These programs incorporate the various aspects of health, physical, recreational and leisure activities necessary for the ultimate goal of a sound mind in a sound body. The concept of a sound mind, sound body constitute the foundation of a happy, productive life. In the United States, interest in the dual goals of sound mind and sound body has burgeoned, spawning a vast array of "wellness" programs, or programs concentrating on health, physical education, recreation and dance (HPRD). But HPRD programs for adults traditionally have focused on the physical and psychosociological needs of young or middle-aged adults; older adults—in some ways the neediest group—have often been ignored. Wellness programs are important for all ages. These programs are especially important for older adults who tend to become deconditioned due to lifestyles that are less active.

The fact is that people of all ages may benefit from HPRD programs. Indeed, the elderly may derive the same benefits from HPRD experiences as do younger adults, i.e., increased vitality, better health, improved stamina, heightened self-esteem and increased engagement in life. Programs must be individualized to meet the needs of the participants and must involve the elements which promote a sound mind in a sound body.

Older individuals have some unique needs that effect the type of wellness programs planned for them. Aging involves a decrease in a person's ability to adapt to his/her environment. It becomes increasingly difficult for the older person to adjust to the many changes that occur in life. Through good health management practices and physical activities, adapting to change becomes easier for the older adult.

Older adults are often concerned with moving efficiently and with the least energy necessary; unfortunately, such a sedentary lifestyle has had a deconditioning affect in many instances. In the section entitled physical needs of the elderly, the functional capacities of the cardiovascular and respiratory systems, changes in the skin, bones, and muscles, and alterations in the nervous system will be discussed.

In addition, older individuals have some unique needs requiring the attention of HPRD professionals. Age-related changes in bodily structures and functions, combined with a tendency toward sedentary living, have a generally deconditioning effect on many older persons. Physical fitness, defined for the elderly person as the ability to perform daily chores with energy left for recreational and social activities (P.C.P.F.S., 1973), tends to deteriorate. As will be shown, HPRD programs tailored to individual needs can increase fitness and even forestall some physical declines associated with aging.

The President's Council on Physical Fitness describes two aspects of physical fitness: organic fitness and dynamic fitness. Organic fitness refers to a body free of disease or infirmity and well-nourished. Dynamic fitness refers to the ability to move vigorously and live in an energetic manner. The sedentary lifestyle of most older adults is a major cause of the loss of dynamic fitness. Components of dynamic fitness would include cardiovascular composition (P.C.P.F.S., 1973). When discussing the musculature, skeleton, and nervous system of the human body and their involvement in movement, the major concern of this manuscript will be the effects of aging on changes in these systems.

This monograph will also discuss the application of HPRD to other health considerations of the elderly, such as stress, nutrition and weight control, smoking, and drug interaction. A variety of recreational, leisure, and physical activities that encourage good health management techniques which will decrease feelings of mental strain and provide a socially enjoyable environment will also be discussed.

The HPRD profession can also help older adults manage some of the psychosociological aspects of growing old. Adjustment to declining socioeconomic status, loneliness, and reduced mobility, for example, may be eased through carefully designed HPRD experiences.

Thus, the purpose of this document is to describe some of the physical, sociological, and psychological characteristics of older adults, identify their needs, and outline the role of the HPRD profession in meeting those needs. The monograph will describe several wellness programs that are helping older individuals live healthier, happier lives. Finally, the document suggests ways of initiating and maintaining good health management practices, including exercise and diversified leisure activities, especially for those who have been sedentary for several years or more.

The HPRD profession can play a key role in improving the quality of the lives of elderly persons. In the past, ignorance and inexperience have limited the efforts of the profession to extend itself to this growing group of citizens. HPRD specialists must now help to correct society's long neglect of the elderly by working to understand and reach out to older Americans.

I

Definition of the Elderly and Theories of Aging

CLASSIFICATION OF THE ELDERLY

In order to define the elderly population it is important to understand their behavior. The age stratification model is a relatively new approach to explaining the behavior of the elderly.

Age is a variable that dictates the number of roles and options that are available to an individual. For example, a young girl cannot play the role of a mother until she is biologically capable. Age is often described in two manners, by chronological age and cohort age.

Chronological age can influence role performance through legal, social, or biological restrictions. Chronological age separates the population into age categories and dictates many of the rights, roles, opportunities, and responsibilities individuals will experience throughout life. For example, in the American society when an individual reaches 65 years of age he or she has the right to collect Social Security. However, at this same age he/she may be forced to retire by mandatory retirement laws.

Cohort age distinguishes individuals by their time of birth. It refers to a group of individuals who were born at about the same time and who experienced specific historical events at about the same age. For example, World War I had long-term effects on the individuals who experienced that part of history. However, the effects were different for those who were 5, 15, 20, or 80 years at the time of World War I. Also, different birth cohorts affect behavior by producing different expectations of the same role. In the past, the role of mother has been to stay within the household to raise and care for the children; but in recent years that has changed and now many mothers also work outside the home.

The elderly population is often divided simply into two categories according to chronological age: the young-old (55-75 years) and the old-old (75 years and over) (Smith & Gilligan, 1983). But great individual variations exist within these two groups, detracting from the usefulness of this means of categorization. Older adults have also been classified by

1

physical ability into the well elderly and the frail elderly. However, here again, great variation exists within the categories. Reports of the fitness levels of older adults range from the 65-year-old competitive athlete to the 65-year-old invalid. Moreover, characteristics of the 90 percent of older adults who fall between these two extremes lack clear definition (Smith & Gilligan, 1983). For the purposes of this manuscript, the older adult is defined in relation to the physical, social and psychological ability to function in everyday situations. Physical age depends on the information previously discussed; whereas social age refers to the observable social habits of an individual as perceived by other members of society. For example, does a chronologically aged 65-year-old act as expected by society or does he/she act like a 40-year-old? Psychological age deals with how well one adapts to environmental demands in comparison with others in society.

In order to understand the various reasons for the classification of elderly, it is imperative to address the different aging theories. Theories of aging strive to provide a more comprehensive, coherent understanding of growing old than is afforded by statistics. Given the paucity of research identifying clearly those factors that influence the rate of aging, theories of aging tend to focus on causes. Biological theories address the basic cellular mechanisms of aging; psychosociological theories address the general welfare of the elderly.

BIOLOGICAL THEORIES OF AGING

Biological theories of aging are based on three principles: first, that the aging phenomenon is universal; it originates within the organism; it occurs gradually. In addition, nearly all biological theories stem from the idea that genetic information within cells is ultimately responsible for maintaining cell function. Most biological theories of aging focus on muscle and nerve cells which are nonreproducing and most clearly show the effects of aging. The biological theories include the cross-linkage theory, wear-and-tear theory, and error theory.

Cross-Linkage Theory

Johan Bjorkoten's cross-linkage theory first described in 1942, associates cross-linking with many of the secondary causes of aging (Rockstein & Sussman, 1979). Cross-linking refers to the formation of chemical bonds between chains of polymer-type molecular structures called amino acids. Some cross-linking is necessary in order to maintain correct biological function of proteins (mainly collagen) and nucleic acids. However, when cross-linkage reaches extreme levels, cell behavior is altered, since the intracellular transport responsible for protein synthesis and immunological function is impeded.

One of the primary causes of cross-linking has been related to a protein known as collagen. This protein aids in building the framework of the lungs, heart, muscle and the inner lining of the blood vessels. It is believed that the ability of collagen to bind with essential molecules diminishes with age and results in decreased flexibility and efficiency of the heart to pump. Cross-linking has also been related to the precise amount of free-radicals formed with the cell. Free-radicals arise as a by-product of normal cell functions involving oxygen. They can cause the formation of a protein in inactive molecules and increase the amount of unsaturated fats in the cell. The unsaturated fat combines with the inactive protein to form a substance known as "lipofusion" or "age pigment," commonly found in aged cardiac and skeletal muscle cells.

Wear-and-Tear Theory

Another biological theory which is closely related to cross-linking deals specifically with cell death or the wearing out of a cell. It suggests that cells are destroyed as a result of an accumulation of chemical by-products of cellular metabolism. The accumulation of these by-products damage the cell contents with age and inhibits repair of damaged vital cellular components; this process can lead to cell death. Organelles such as the mitochondria, endoplasmic reticulum, lysomes, and nuclei have shown these changes in structure and content over time. The mitochondria and cytoplasm alter in size and shape, which reduces their functional capacity in the cell. These cellular changes which occur with age are significantly different than those which occur as a result of injury.

Error Theory

Alterations in the chemical structure of molecules has an effect on the aging process. The molecule of most concern in aging is DNA, deoxyribonucleic acid, since it governs the body build, height, eye, hair, and skin color, and susceptibilities to many diseases and aging mechanisms. When DNA is damaged, as a result of incomplete protein synthesis, to an unrepairable extent death of the cell may occur. DNA along with RNA, ribonucleic acid, are responsible for the production of specific enzymes which carry out all the chemical reactions of the body. These protein enzymes are composed of amino acids, some of which are manufactured in the body. However, there are eight essential amino acids which are not synthesized in the body. These amino acids must be provided from the environment through the ingestion of carbohydrates, lipids, and vitamins. The body does have the capacity to manufacture certain nutrients. However, other raw materials and bodily resources are utilized in the manufacturing process. It is imperative that the body is supplied with the correct amount of nutrients so the chain of chemical reaction functions properly, and to replenish the chemical structure of the cells. Therefore, this theory addresses the question of aging on the basis of time related failure of protein synthesis.

PSYCHOSOCIOLOGICAL THEORIES
OF AGING

Psychosociological theories of aging deal with the general welfare of the elderly and address nonphysical factors that influence the aging process. Included are the influence of society on the elderly and how older adults' perception of themselves influences their thinking about aging. In contrast to biological theories, which focus on physical change, psychosociological theories deal with the elderly's emotional or social needs.

Disengagement Theory

Disengagement is a process whereby individuals withdraw from society. For older adults, it may begin as they are phased out of important roles in order for society to maintain productivity. The phase-out also protects society from the sudden loss of elderly through death. Disengagement is believed to be inevitable; however, the degree and nature of the disengagement vary with differences in health and personality.

Disengagement is believed to be perpetuated by three factors. First, with increasing age, the number and societal importance of a person's roles gradually decline. Examples of such a phenomenon are the decrease in the parental role as children mature and the decline in the work role after retirement. Such a phenomenon does not take place at one time; rather, it is a gradual process.

Secondly, the current structure of society may encourage disengagement by imposing restrictions on the behavior of the elderly. For instance, some states require the older person to take a driving test every year in order to retain a license. Finally, disengagement may afford mutual satisfaction to society and the elderly. When an older individual disengages, his or her role is filled by a younger individual; often, the older individual is happy to escape the demands and pressures of former roles.

The disengagement theory became prominent in 1960 with the so-called Kansas City Studies. These studies were based on a cross-sectional survey analysis of 275 people ranging in age from 50–90. The results of these studies (Cumming & Henry, 1961) suggested that older adults became more selective in their roles with increasing age and there was a significant decline in the number of current roles, current role activity, ego involvement in current roles and in societal interaction. It was suggested that these declines were logical, natural, normal and satisfying (Teaff, 1985). On the other hand, some studies suggest that disengagement is largely a result of lack of opportunities for the elderly, poor health, loss of friends, or reduced families (Maddox, 1963; Rose, 1964; Carp, 1968).

Activity Theory

The activity theory was formulated to demonstrate the weakness of the disengagement theory. The theory is based upon the belief that a decrease in activity corresponds with a decrease in life satisfaction. Activity theorists claim that happiness is achieved by maintaining middle-aged ways of life, values, and beliefs for as long as possible. This is accomplished by replacing lost roles or relationships, something the elderly, for a variety of physical and social reasons, cannot always do.

In opposition to activity theory, some researchers have found that high morale is not dependent on the number of roles an individual has, but rather on having stable, enduring relationships (Lemon, Bengtson, Peterson, 1972).

Subculture Theory

A subculture refers to a group within the general society that holds the same cultural characteristics as society while exhibiting characteristics unique to the group. The subculture theory poses the existence of an older adult subculture, a recent phenomenon that has evolved partly as a result of an increase in the elderly population. This increase has led to older adults forming a group with its own ideas, beliefs, values, and behaviors. In addition, the elderly are often forced to decrease participation in society due to health problems or retirement laws, thus intensifying their isolation. Age consciousness is another factor; the elderly are recognizing that they possess common interests and needs that unite them as a subculture.

Subculture theorists believe that the older adult subculture is more powerful than other subcultures, to which the elderly may belong, such as ethnic, religious, or occupational groups (Crandall, 1980). However, not all elderly persons attach themselves to the older adult subculture in the same way. Factors such as health, income, education, and family responsibilities affect the importance of the subculture to each person. This creates the possibility of subsubcultures within the older adult subculture. For example, wealthy elderly individuals possess different values and beliefs than do destitute elderly individuals. Each group may form a subsubculture with those in the same category.

Role Theory

Role theorists think of "older adult" as a role to which society attaches certain expectations (Crandall, 1980). To an extent, these theorists believe the older individual's behavior is determined by the "older adult" role

5

with its enjoining norms. However, most norms allow some flexibility. For example, the role of "mother" may suggest a certain behavior in our society, but no two mothers behave exactly the same way.

Role theory maintains that several factors affect the behavior of older adults within the "older adult" role. One such factor is the guidance provided by persons in positions of authority or influence: mother, teacher, boss, coach, husband. These individuals may alter the behavior of others through the use of reward and punishment.

Another factor in performance or behavior is the roles of those with whom we interact and the ways in which the individuals in those roles behave. For example, an elderly person may behave in a certain manner when in the presence of a coworker; their behavior may change in the presence of a boss. Also, one may have to change behavior with the same individual. A person's apparent mood, for example, may affect coworkers' behavior toward that person.

Feedback is another factor that affects behavior. When feedback from associates indicates acceptance of an individual's behavior, the behavior is reinforced. On the other hand, if the response is negative, the behavior will likely change.

The last factor influencing role behavior is the individual's interpretation of the role according to his or her personality and socialization. For example, the role of grandparent is interpreted differently by each individual, resulting in infinite variation in the behavior of individuals in that role.

Labeling Theory

This theory resembles role theory in its view that society's labeling of people can influence their behavior. Labeling theory suggests that once a label such as "old" is given to an individual, it has a significant impact on the way in which society perceives and reacts to that individual. Once applied, labels resist modification and a certain "master status" develops. This status overrides all other statuses achieved by the individual. Initially, the labeled individual may not accept the connotations associated with the label. However, eventually, the label is incorporated into the behavior of the individual, as society reinforces him or her for behaving in the manner it associates with the label. Thus, the individual experiences a reduction in the number of role options.

Phenomenological Theory

This theory holds that older persons' behavior is determined largely by their individual perceptions of the world, perceptions shaped in part by socialization and experience. For example, older adults react differently to retirement. The differences are viewed not as the result of the phenomenon of retirement itself, but as the interpretation of the phenomenon by each individual.

The phenomenological theory accounts for perceptual differences among individuals from the same age group. For example, two individuals may have experienced the Depression at the same age. However, for one of the individuals it may have brought severe struggle; for the other, only minor changes in lifestyle.

Each of the preceding theories of aging aids in the understanding of the elderly. Biological theories explain the physiological changes experienced by most individuals, while the psychosociological theories bring into focus how and why the elderly differ from other groups and from each other.

Society tends to address only the biological theories, which means that nature is seen as accounting for most of the changes that take place in the older adult. This is not true in most cases, since psychosociological changes play just as much of a role. It is difficult to understand the developmental changes which take place in the elderly. Many societal attitudes toward the elderly are based on myths. It is important for the fitness director to be able to sort fact from fiction when considering the older adult.

CURRENT STATUS OF THE ELDERLY

To a great extent, our attitudes about aging are dominated by myths, stereotypes, and ignorance. As myths color our perception of the elderly, the elderly alter their perception of themselves (Schaie & Geiwitz, 1982). Recent research provides a more realistic portrait of the elderly in terms of economic status, health, geographic location, ethnic and racial composition.

One myth is that the older population becomes more and more dependent on society to fulfill their basic needs. On the contrary, research indicates that 95 percent of the elderly live independently or with their immediate families (Ringler, 1982). In regard to marital status, about 79 percent of older males are married and 39 percent of older females are married. Due to the fact that many women are widows, older women are more likely than older men to live alone (Harris, 1978).

The present health status of the elderly is a major factor influencing the behavior and involvement of the elderly within the community. Another common myth is that most people over 65 years of age are unhealthy. In reality, research indicates that 8 in 10 persons aged 65 or over describe their health as "good" or "excellent," compared with others of their age (Taeuber, 1983). However, good health is often associated with higher incomes: Forty percent of those claiming good health had annual incomes exceeding $25,000, while less than one quarter of those earning $7,000 or less reported excellent health (U.S. Department of Health and Human Services, in press).

Another myth concerning the elderly is the belief that older people experience intellectual deterioration and cannot benefit from education. This assumption cannot be applied to the older population in general. When addressing intellectual ability, it is important to consider physical and social factors. Research indicates that intellectual abilities dealing with verbal factors and stored information decline by a relatively small amount with increasing age (Crandall, 1980). The small percentage of decline in intellectual ability is due to cell degeneration and death.

In the past, knowledge was associated with experience; therefore, the older adult was considered more knowledgeable than a younger individual. In today's society, knowledge is associated with the recent advances in technology and it is the young individual who has made these advances. Since the elderly have been denied the opportunity to engage in the current educational system, they are often thought of as being educationally inferior. In 1980, the average years of schooling completed by an older person was 10.2. Of that total population, 41 percent completed high school, while only 9 percent completed college (U.S. Department of Health and Human Services, 1980–1981). If the elderly population has support from the general society to pursue their education, they can achieve great gains. Older adults are capable of high levels of learning, given proper incentives.

In 1982, about 12 percent of whites, 8 percent of blacks, 6 percent of Asians and Pacific Islanders, 5 percent of American Indians, and 5 percent of Hispanics were 65 years of age and older. Between 1970–1980, the elderly white population grew by about 25 percent and the elderly black population by 33 percent (U.S. Bureau of the Census, 1983).

Economic well being is a major concern for all adults, but especially for the elderly. For 91.2 percent of this population, the major source of income is social security (Taeuber, 1983). It accounts for 37 percent of the total income of elderly persons; earnings, property income, and pensions are found to be of varying significance (Taeuber, 1983). The income of the elderly is associated with many factors that the elderly person cannot control—sex, health of spouse, and their own health. It is estimated that the median income in 1981 of men aged 60 to 64 years was about $15,000; however, income decreased dramatically to $8,200 for men aged 65. Women, who tend to earn less than men throughout life, follow much the same pattern, with the exception that the decline begins at age 50 (Taeuber, 1983). Economic status has an important influence on the older person's quality of life. Low income in old age often means inadequate housing and clothing, poor nutrition, lack of recreation, and neglect of medical and health needs (Teaff, 1985).

In the period of 1980–81, doctors' leading diagnoses for the elderly were hypertension, diabetes, chronic ischemic heart disease, cataracts, and osteoarthritis (U.S. Department of Health and Human Services, 1980–81). Many of these conditions were also leading causes for limitation of activity. The improvement of these health factors is imperative to the elderly population. Improvement of health behaviors can also decrease the cost of health care. It is estimated that health care expenditures not covered by Medicare consume an average of 19.9 percent of all yearly income for those 65 and over (Senate Special Committee on Aging Staff, 1977).

Another factor that influences the lifestyle of the elderly is geographical location. Almost half of the elderly population resides in seven states: California, New York, Pennsylvania, Texas, Illinois, Ohio, and Florida (Ringler, 1982). In 1981, almost two-thirds of the elderly population lived in metropolitan areas. However, the size of the elderly population in small towns and rural areas has increased about 2.5 percent annually in recent years (Ringler, 1982). With increasing age, people move less often; most older persons remain in the same location and most of the elderly who did relocate between 1975 and 1980 stayed within the same metropolitan area (Ringler, 1982).

Research shows that the way people age is affected by their economic status, educational level, health status, and geographical location (Ringler, 1982). The rate of aging may also be affected by the satisfaction of the basic needs.

II

Needs of the Older Adult

All people have certain physical and emotional needs in common. Clearly, everyone needs food, water, and shelter, for example, as well as companionship, attention, and other forms of emotional nourishment. For the older adult, however, the mosaic of needs shifts; certain needs loom larger or take on new dimensions.

Maslow's Hierarchy of Needs

The basic physical and psychosociological needs for the elderly population can be best exemplified by Maslow's Hierarchy of Needs. In this theory, the lowest needs on the hierarchy must be satisfied before higher needs are attainable. Maslow's Hierarchical Theory states that physiological needs are the lowest and most basic needs for an individual, followed by needs for safety and security, social interaction, esteem, and self-actualization (Schaie & Geiwitz, 1982).

Under physiological needs, the older adult is concerned with survival which includes the need for water, food, air, and shelter. Safety and security needs of an older adult deals with security and protection from physical and emotional harm. Some examples may include freedom from fear of intruders to their home, falling and not being able to get up, and being battered by their own children upon whom they have become dependent. To achieve safety, elderly individuals form groups for mutual security and protection.

Next in the hierarchy are social needs. Human beings have a basic need for friendship and companionship. The need for self-esteem in the older adult involves the achievement of status within a group, recognition, and attention. Individuals need the respect of others as well as self-respect. After these four needs are met, the need for self-actualization emerges. The self-actualizing individual is the architect of his own destiny and self-fulfillment. It is the self-actualizing person who tries to reach his/her fullest potential in all activities he/she undertakes. This is particularly difficult for the older adult because of the negative attitude many people have toward aging (Schaie & Geiwitz, 1982).

Physical Needs

As previously mentioned, wellness programs deal with all of Maslow's needs and any physical limitations and/or changes which might take place in the aging process. Maslow considers the physical needs of an individual the most basic in his hierarchy. HPRD programs for older adults must take into account the physical limitations and changes that can occur as adults age. Changes in the functional capacities of the cardiovascular, respiratory, skeletal, musculature, and nervous systems will be covered. Nutritional needs will also be discussed. Aging is a process of change in the physical powers and capacities of the human body. Gradual improvement in the physical functions of the body occurs until approximately 17 years of age. From that time until age 26, relatively minor changes occur. After that, the physical capacities of the body generally decline for the remainder of the life span (Clark, 1977). Indeed, HPRD programs should strive to educate the elderly concerning such physical changes and help them adapt (Leviton & Campanelli, 1980). In addition, HPRD programs can develop individualized programs for the older adult to slow and even prevent some of these changes.

Cardiovascular System. One factor in the aging process is a decrease in the ability of the cardiovascular system to supply the body with enough blood for efficient function. A constant blood flow provides the body with the necessary amounts of oxygen and nutrients while removing waste products. The heart must be able to pump blood adequately. The rate at which the heart pumps (heart rate) and the quantity of blood released with each stroke (stroke volume) determine cardiac output (McArdle, Katch & Katch, 1981). Put another way, cardiac output is the amount of blood pumped by the heart in a unit period of time (Guyton, 1981).

Because it varies with body size, cardiac output may be described in terms of the cardiac index. The cardiac index is a measure of the cardiac output per square meter of body surface area. At 10 years of age, the cardiac index is slightly greater than 4 liters per minute per square meter; at 80 years, the index declines to 2.4 liters per minute per square meter (Guyton, 1981). In a resting condition, low cardiac output in the elderly results from reduced stroke volume and a normal heart rate. During light work, cardiac output is much like that of a younger person. However, as work increases, the stroke volume of an elderly person diminishes 10 to 20 percent compared to a younger adult (Shepard, 1981). There are many causes for decreased cardiac output and cardiac index in an older adult, resulting in decreased blood supply to tissues. Hypertension, coronary heart disease, fabrotic changes in the vascular system, and loss of blood-vessel elasticity all may restrict cardiac output (Guyton, 1981).

Hypertension or high blood pressure is one of the major causes of cardiovascular disease (Miller & Allen, 1979). Blood pressure may be

11

altered if there is a change in the cardiac output of the heart due to an increase in the rigidity in the vascular walls of the arteries and veins or an obstruction of blood flow through the vascular system (Guyton, 1981). At rest, normal blood pressure for a young adult is 120/80 mm Hg (hemoglobin) (McArdle, Katch, & Katch, 1981). For adults over 60 years of age, average blood pressure, reported from the Cooper Clinic Coronary Risk Factor Profile Charts, is 130/80 mm Hg for women and 131/81 mm Hg for men (Pollack, Wilmore, & Fox, 1978). The first number represents systolic pressure; the bottom number, the diastolic pressure. Systolic pressure is a measure of the work of the heart and the strain against arterial walls during a ventricular contraction. The diastolic pressure is a measure of the relaxation phase of the heart during the cardiac cycle. The diastolic pressure measures the ease with which blood flows from the arterioles to the capillaries (Pollack, Wilmore, & Fox, 1978). Borderline hypertension for the older adult, as reported in the 1971–1974 Health and Nutrition Examination Survey, ranges from 140/90 to 160/95 mm Hg. Definite hypertension according to the survey begins at a reading of 160/95 mm Hg (U.S. Department of Health and Human Services, 1981). As adults age, systolic pressure may rise by 10 to 40 percent. Diastolic pressure hypertensive limits may lead to complications of the cardiovascular system in older adults due to chronic or continuous stress on the cardiovascular system (McArdle, Katch, & Katch, 1981).

Coronary heart disease is caused by degeneration of the inner lining of the large arteries that supply the heart. These blood vessels may become lined with lipid or fat filled plaques, fibrous scar tissue, or both. Congested vessels restrict blood flow to the heart muscle, thereby reducing cardiac output. When this occurs, the heart (myocardium) becomes ischemic due to a poor supply of oxygen. The condition of increased cholesterol plaques or fatty substances causing arterial congestion is called atherosclerosis; when calcium joins with these lipids, calcified plaques form causing hardening of the arteries, or arteriosclerosis (Guyton, 1981). The degenerative process of atherosclerosis may cause slow flowing blood to clot (thrombus) and plug a coronary blood vessel. When this occurs, a portion of the heart muscle dies due to loss of oxygen, and the individual experiences a heart attack (myocardial infarction). Death from coronary heart disease usually occurs when several major blood vessels supplying the heart are severely constricted. When blood is not totally constricted but falls below requirements, an individual may experience chest pains called angina pectoris (McArdle, Katch, & Katch, 1981). Other problems associated with atherosclerosis are: a decrease in heart rate in response to stress placed on the heart; a decrease in the efficiency of the heart as a pump; a loss of elasticity in the arteries and veins; and an increase or decrease in blood pressure from normal levels in some individuals (a decrease in blood

12

pressure may occur due to a decrease in cardiac output) (Leviton & Campanelli, 1980).

Coronary heart disease is the number one cause of death in the western world. Research indicates that twice as many people die from coronary heart disease as from cancer. It has also been found that between the ages of 55 and 65, 13 out of every 100 males and 6 out of every 100 females die from coronary heart disease (McArdle, Katch, & Katch, 1981).

Respiratory System. The ability of the lungs to take in oxygen and exhale carbon dioxide is termed external respiration. The ability of the body to exchange oxygen and carbon dioxide between the blood supply and cells of the body is termed internal respiration (Rockstein & Sussman, 1979). The maximum amount of oxygen that can be used by the body is the single best measure of changes in the respiratory system (Bruce, 1984).

With advancing age, changes take place in the rib cage and air passageways that result in a decrease in the ability of the body to inhale and exhale air. Cartilage connecting the ribs to the spinal column and the sternum begins to stiffen from calcification lessening the ability of the rib cage to expand. The stiffening of the cartilage may also cause kyphosis, a forward curvature of the spine in the thoracic area. Osteoporosis, or softening of the bone, may also contribute to kyphosis due to a collapse of the vertebral column. Kyphosis reduces the area in which the lungs can expand making breathing more difficult (Rockstein & Sussman, 1979).

Calcification of the cartilage in the trachea and bronchi decreases the ability of the lungs to expand and contract while inhaling and exhaling. This phenomenon also causes a decrease in the ability of the body to use oxygen. From ages 25 to 85, the maximum breathing capacity declines 55 to 60 percent as contractability of the rib cage and air passageways declines (Rockstein & Sussman, 1979).

The lungs may also lose elasticity. As the amount of collagen in the lungs decreases, the ability of the air sacs in the lungs to expand declines, impairing internal respiration. Emphysema is a disease of the lungs that is related to both the age and lifestyle of the individual. This degenerative disease causes collagen in the walls of the aveoli or air sacs to give way to fibrous tissue. This reduces the respiratory surface of the lungs and lowers maximum breathing capacity (Rockstein & Sussman, 1979).

The average rate of respiration changes little with age. In a waking rest state, old and young adults both take between 12 and 14 breaths per minute (Rockstein & Sussman, 1979). Tidal volume, or the total amount of air moved while inhaling or exhaling, also changes little as an individual ages. The minute respiratory volume, a measure of air moving into and out of the lungs per minute, is a product of the respiratory rate and tidal volume and remains fairly constant with age. However, the efficiency of oxygen and carbon dioxide exchange in the lungs may decrease because of a loss of lung elasticity (Guyton, 1981).

The maximum amount of air an individual can forcibly expire is called their vital capacity (McArdle, Katch, & Katch, 1981). Because of declining contractibility of the chest cavity and lungs vital capacity may decline by 40 to 50 percent from age 30 to 70 (Smith & Gilligan, 1983). With decreased vital capacity comes increased residual air volume, the amount of air that is not exhaled and remains in the lungs. Residual volume may increase 30 to 50 percent from age 30 to 70 years (Smith & Gilligan, 1983).

Due to a decreased functional capacity of the lungs and a lower immunity to infection as one grows older, respiratory infections, such as chronic bronchitis, tuberculosis, and pneumonia become more common. Cigarette smoke and air pollution may also contribute to respiratory problems (Rockstein & Sussman, 1979).

Skin, Bones, and Muscles. The most readily observable physical changes associated with aging are those of the skin, bones, and muscles. Loss or graying of the hair is common; fingernails may become brittle and start to turn yellow; the skin may wrinkle, dry, and sag. Of course, alterations in the skin may occur in response both to aging and environmental elements (Rockstein & Sussman, 1979).

The epidermis, or outer layer of the skin, decreases in its ability of cell division with age resulting in slow healing processes. From age 27 to 65, there is an 80 percent decrease in pigment cells (melanocytes) in the epidermis. Those pigment cells that remain tend to become larger and some may appear as "age spots." In the dermis, or deeper layer of the skin, supplies of collagen, fat, and water decline and cause elastic fibers to become cross-linked and calcified. Changes, such as these in the skin, cause sagging and wrinkling (Rockstein & Sussman, 1979).

Degeneration of the bone is a major concern related to aging. Decreases of calcium and phosphate as a result of poor nutrition, may cause bones to become porous and brittle. Osteoporosis is an extreme condition to which the increased occurrence of bone fractures in older adults may be related. A decrease in the stability of the spinal column may also occur with age.

Research has shown that bone loss in aging is greater in women than in men (Rockstein & Sussman, 1979). In the average, female bone loss begins around 35 to 40 years of age. By age 70, women have lost as must as 25 to 30 percent of their bone mass. Men begin to lose bone mass around 55 years of age with a 15 to 20 percent loss by age 70 (Smith & Gilligan, 1983).

Lessened mobility in older adults is associated with a decrease in muscle mass—both the size and number of muscle fibers. Muscular strength

14

declines with age due to a decrease in muscle mass, along with the speed at which a muscle can contract and relax during movement (Edington & Edgerton, 1976). Changes that occur in muscles vary according to their use in physical activities. The length of an individual's inactivity and the rate of degeneration of the muscles determine the level of deconditioning or atrophy (a decrease in muscle mass) that takes place (Rockstein & Sussman, 1979).

As the size of the muscle decreases there may be an increase in the fat and collagen content of the muscle and a resulting loss of muscle elasticity. The elastic component of muscles aid in the mechanical support of the body. Elastic fibers allow muscle tissue to yield to external forces and then return to original shape when the forces are removed (Adrian, 1981).

Flexibility is defined as the ability of an individual to move the body joints through a maximum range of motion. In aging, a decrease in flexibility attends a decrease in muscle elasticity. Along with the muscles, the tendons, ligaments, and cartilage surrounding the various joints of the body also lose elasticity decreasing the joints' range of motion (Jenson & Schultz, 1977; Adrian, 1981).

Loss of balance and coordination during movement may accompany declining strength and flexibility. Older persons may avoid simple daily movements such as walking and climbing stairs for fear of injury. Lifelong habits of inactivity, combined with impaired movement and well meant admonitions to "slow down and take it easy" may produce hypokinetic syndrome in a large portion of the elderly population. Hypokinesis refers to a low amount of movement and exercise along with inadequate energy expenditure due to lack of movement (Munns, 1981). Such a condition may lead to such problems as poor circulation and obesity.

Arthritis is a common ailment of the elderly that may further restrict movement. It generally consists of inflammation, pain, and stiffness of one or more joints, often the ankles, knees, hips, shoulders, wrists, or fingers (Munns, 1981). Approximately 4 percent of men and 23 percent of women over the age of 45 have some form of arthritis.

Arthritis has three common forms: rheumatoid arthritis, osteoarthritis, and gout (Leviton & Campanelli, 1980). Rheumatoid arthritis involves deterioration of joints along with the muscles and tendons surrounding the joints. It is a crippling disease most common between the ages of 20 and 50. Osteoarthritis typically afflicts the elderly population. It is described as a chronic inflammation of the cartilage of the joints resulting in swelling, stiffness, and pain. Gout results from an impaired ability of the body to eliminate uric acid during metabolism. Excess uric acid in the body combines with sodium forming urate crystals. These crystals are deposited into soft tissue of the joints causing swelling, inflammation, and pain.

Gout has been linked to diet and environmental factors such as stress and climate (Tortora, 1977).

Nervous System. Age related changes in the nervous system are important in considering the physical needs of the older adult. The nervous system, central and autonomic, coordinates the activities of all other systems. The autonomic nervous system functions at a subconscious level and controls many functions of the heart, liver, and stomach. The autonomic nervous system is composed of parasympathetic and sympathetic divisions which carry the impulses to the organs. Control of energy expenditure and coping with stressful activities are the major concerns of the sympathetic system, while the parasympathetic system controls activities that store and conserve energy in the body. For example, the parasympathetic nervous system may slow or weaken the force of the heartbeat, while the sympathetic nervous system may quicken or increase the force of the heartbeat (Rockstein & Sussman, 1979).

The central nervous system is comprised of the brain and spinal cord. The brain can generate thought, retain information, and determine how the body should respond to specific situations. Appropriate signals are then guided through the motor section of the nervous system to perform the person's desires. Age may also alter the structure and function of nerve cells, causing some to shrink, others to swell. Nerve cells do not regenerate; therefore, when these cells die as an individual ages, they are not replaced. One cause of death of a nerve cell is lipofusion or the accumulation of yellowish fat pigments which join the outer lining of the brain. A loss in the amount of nerve fiber with increasing age may be related to a decrease in the rate of conduction of messages from one nerve to another (Rockstein & Sussman, 1979). In men and women between the ages of 30 and 70, nerve conduction velocity may decrease by 10 to 15 percent (Smith & Gilligan, 1983), reducing the speed of reaction to the environment (Rockstein & Sussman, 1979).

Aging in the central nervous system is related to a decrease in brain mass. In extreme cases, the loss of brain mass may be as much as 20 percent. Some research indicates a 7 to 27 percent reduction in the verbal ability, the ability to store information and then recall the information in order to speak, of an elderly person compared with verbal ability of a 30-year-old. Motor performance may also decline 26 to 50 percent (Rockstein & Sussman, 1979).

Advancing age can also affect an individual's memory. Older adults tend to remember events that took place in the relatively distant past (long-term memory) more clearly than recent events (short-term memory). Senility is the term often used to describe memory loss in the elderly. Researchers have not discovered the actual cause of memory loss, but some have suggested that it may be related to the motivation and attitudes

16

of the elderly as well as to the age-related physical changes (Rockstein & Sussman, 1979). Studies suggest that well-educated, mentally active people do not exhibit the same decline (Botwinick, 1973).

A buildup of fatty substances in the arteries of the brain reduces the ability of the blood to supply oxygen and nutrients to the brain and may result in a stroke, a fairly common problem among the elderly. Eighty percent of all strokes are caused by the formation of clots or an increase of fatty deposits in the arteries of the brain; 20 percent hemorrhaging of blood vessels in the brain. The degree of neural impairment following a stroke depends upon the severity of the stroke. Many times those who survive a stroke may require long term rehabilitation therapy in order to reverse an associated loss in neurological capabilities, particularly in regard to mobility and communication (Rockstein & Sussman, 1979).

Aging of the autonomic nervous system is associated with an increase in the period of time it takes for the heart rate and respiratory volume to return to normal after physical activity. The system's ability to respond to environmental stress declines with age. For example, some older adults have difficulty maintaining normal body temperature when the temperature in their environment falls below 68 degrees Farenheit. Changes in bowel and bladder function may also result from age related alterations in the autonomic nervous system (Rockstein & Sussman, 1979).

The Senses. Aging also affects the sensory cells and organs responsible for seeing, hearing, tasting, smelling and touching. Normally, for example, advancing age brings a decrease in the size of the pupil of the eye (Rockstein & Sussman, 1979), impairing the eye's ability to adapt to darkness and increasing the intensity of light needed in order to see. Cataracts are common in the elderly population. An individual with cataracts has blurred or glared vision caused by the lens of the eye becoming opaque. Surgery and corrective lenses may enhance vision in cataract patients. Presbyopia (farsightedness) and decreased peripheral vision and depth perception may also affect the older individual's vision (Rockstein & Sussman, 1979).

Hearing loss, while known to occur in men and women of all age groups, is most common between the ages of 55 and 75. In fact, over 27 percent of the population over age 74 has impaired hearing. Excessive noise, disease, certain drugs, or loss of nerve cells in the inner ear all may cause hearing loss, generally of high pitches. This difficulty causes problems in word discrimination and in locating the sources of sounds. Hearing loss is often associated with slurred speech, and difficulty in monitoring speech volume (Rockstein & Sussman, 1979).

Although research concerning age-related changes in physical structures responsible for tasting and smelling is scant, it is known that the number of taste buds diminishes as an individual ages, decreasing the sensitivity of taste receptors. An additional factor that lessens taste sen-

17

sitivity is a decline in the flow of saliva. In cases of severe loss in the sense of taste, appetite may be lost (Rockstein & Sussman, 1979).

Because the sense of smell enhances attraction to food, its loss may inhibit appetite in the same way declining sensitivity to taste can. Certainly, the number of nerve cell endings in the nasal cavity that detect smell decreases with age. Inability to detect dangerous gases and smoke is a major concern (Rockstein & Sussman, 1979).

Sensitivity to touch declines up to approximately 60 years of age as nerve impulse receptors in the skin decrease in number. However, at approximately 70 or 80 years of age, individuals may begin to experience heightened tactile sensitivity as loss of skin uncovers nerve endings. In very old adults, the decline in sensitivity to pain may result in an inability to feel a cut or burn that requires medical attention. Consequently, such injuries may become infected and lead to additional health problems (Rockstein & Sussman, 1979).

Nutrition. Proper nutritional habits may forestall some health problems associated with age and generally enhance the health of older adults. Conversely, poor nutrition may precipitate health problems. The types of foods consumed by the elderly individual may affect the ability of the heart to function efficiently. A diet high in cholesterol and triglycerides can lead to an increase in the levels of these fats in the blood stream, a condition known as hyperlipidemia. Evidence links hyperlipidemia with an increase in coronary heart diseases in the adult population. Additional research suggests that the substance that carries these fats in the blood stream—a carrier called a lipoprotein—may have an effect on coronary heart disease (Guyton, 1981). Fats are carried by both high-density lipoproteins (HDLs) and low-density lipoproteins (LDLs). HDLs are excreted by the body. LDLs, however, cannot be metabolized and may accumulate on vascular walls. It is believed that if HDL levels in the blood are above 60 percent, lipid deposits in the arteries will be negligible (Miller & Allen, 1979). The average concentrations of cholesterol, triglycerides, and lipoprotein per 100 milliliters of blood plasma is: 180 milligrams percent for cholesterol, 160 milligrams percent for triglyceride, and 200 milligrams percent for lipoprotein. When the levels of these substances exceed these average concentrations, the risk of coronary heart disease increases (Guyton, 1981).

Salt consumption is another dietary factor that may affect the health of the older person. High salt consumption has been associated with hypertension and an increased risk of coronary heart disease. Little, if any, research claims that an increase in sodium consumption actually produces high blood pressure in an individual who has normal blood pressure. However, hypertensive individuals who reduce their salt intake often show a decline in blood pressure levels (Williams, 1983).

Obesity is another risk factor that may lead to heart and respiratory problems such as atherosclerosis, coronary heart disease, diabetes, and bronchitis in older adults. Overweight may also cause changes in the skin, muscles, and bones that can lead to gout and to accidents resulting from poor balance (Rockstein & Sussman, 1979).

To maintain normal weight, the amount of food consumed by an individual should include just enough energy (calories) to meet daily metabolic needs (Pollack, Wilmore, & Fox, 1978). The basal metabolic rate declines by 5 percent every 10 years between the ages of 35 and 55 and by 8 percent every 10 years between the ages of 55 and 75. Every 10 years after the age of 75 years, the basal metabolic rate decreases an additional 10 percent (Rockstein & Sussman, 1979). In addition, physical activity generally declines with age. Thus, in order to avoid excessive weight gain most people must cut back their calorie intake.

Psychosociological Needs

Once an individual's physical needs are satisfied, he/she can then deal with needs for security, law and order, and freedom from fear, as well as the need for help with various activities. Many of the individuals who withdraw from society become stagnant and find it very difficult to continue to the next level of the hierarchy, which is the need for belongingness and love. At this level, the individual desires meaningful contact with friends, lovers, and children. If these needs are not fulfilled, the individual will experience loneliness. Stress from loneliness harms an individual in certain ways; for example, long-term emotional stress changes the neurochemical processes of the body (Rodgers, 1982). It has been reported that bachelors under age 65 have twice the death rate from cancer and heart disease as married men (Rodgers, 1982).

The last two levels of Maslow's hierarchy deal with self-esteem and self-actualization. Both of these factors are associated with psychological factors of aging. This area of aging is concerned with the understanding and interpreting of behavior as affected by the aging process. It addresses the adaptive changes which occur during the life cycle due to the aging process and also factors independent of aging. When dealing with the psychological needs, it is imperative to investigate the elderly's body image. This refers to how one perceives his/her body and its capabilities to perform. Factors such as wrinkles, tooth loss, handicaps and changes in the tone and texture of the muscle and skin will influence one's body image. These factors can lead to the inability of the elderly to adapt to various life situations, and may also contribute to psychiatric disorders. The most frequent of these disorders is depression, which is a result of many sub-factors such as common worries and loneliness.

The success of these levels in the hierarchy is dependent upon how the attitudes of society influence the behavior of the elderly, along with the various sociological stressors. Aging requires a series of adaptations to unpredictable and predictable stresses. The major sociological stressors that increase with age include separation from family and friends, death, and unwanted changes such as retirement, a decrease in physical capacity, or declining income. A person's ability to adapt to specific stresses, whether predicted or unpredicted, can affect the rate of aging. Predicted stressors consist of planned events such as planned retirement or a planned move to a new home. Unpredicted stressors are often more difficult to handle than predicted stressors, since the individual may not have planned for them. Such events include the death of a spouse, unexpected loss of employment, forced retirement, decline in health, or loss of income.

Retirement, like many of the other events, can produce either a positive or negative stress. The key concept in dealing with stress is perception, since it influences the extent of the response to stress. Retirement can be anticipated as a way to expand and enrich lives in ways one could not while still employed. Retirement can become a negative stress when an individual has no goals in mind for his/her time.

The following section will explain the implications of these needs for HPRD programs for the older adult.

III

How an HPRD Wellness Program Can Meet the Needs of the Elderly

Wellness programs for the elderly are relatively new. Until the 1970s, when a fitness craze exploded in the United States, society in general was ignorant of the benefits of fitness and individualized fitness programs. Today, however, professionals in health, physical education, recreation, and dance are branching out into the field of wellness for the elderly population.

Most professionals involved in HPRD related fields have the basic biological and behavioral science background to conduct activity programs. However, many of these professionals have been involved only with programs devoted to children and young adults. The professional can apply some of this knowledge to older adults, but also needs an understanding of the effects of age on movement patterns and fitness, as described earlier in this monograph. Some basic principles apply to any exercise program; some of these principles, however, may need to be modified in exercise programs directed toward older adults.

The sociological and psychological aspects of aging also help to determine what sorts of HPRD experiences will benefit older clients. Sociological factors include education, religion, economic status, and friendships. Psychological factors may include loss of independence, depression, and loneliness.

One of the most important concerns in any wellness program is motivation. Young people engaging in physical activity may strive for athletic prowess. Older adults, however, have more to contend with physically, and their goals are seldom so lofty, which can make motivation a problem. Many older individuals believe that their need for exercise diminishes and eventually disappears as they age. They vastly exaggerate the risks of vigorous exercise after middle age. They also overrate the benefits of light and sporadic exercise and underrate their abilities.

To overcome these misperceptions, HPRD professionals should emphasize the emotional benefits of regular exercise—a happier, more

21

optimistic outlook; enhanced self-image; better sleep; and less need for stimulants and tranquilizers (Smith & Gilligan, 1983).

It is also essential that the participants determine the goals of the elderly program participants. Often, the goal is to improve motor skills or the ability to pursue everyday tasks without fatigue. Another common goal is to interact with others with the same interest.

HPRD wellness programs should be able to adapt their guidelines to insure that individuals with sensory difficulties can successfully participate in planned activities. Visual changes will limit the physical, recreational, leisure, and dance activities of an older person. The enjoyment of reading, watching television, knitting, or playing cards, may decrease with vision problems possibly making the older person feel isolated from society. Depression may set in due to the feeling of being incapable of participating in various activities. Perceptual tasks such as identifying designs and patterns may take longer with older adults (Shephard, 1978). HPRD activities that are planned should take this into account and provide activities that involve large, bright objects. Also, signs, charts and instructions should be in large, bold print.

Planned HPRD activities must also take into account hearing difficulties of the older adult. Communication is a basic need, and spoken word is a prime means of communication. Hearing loss may be the most isolating sense loss that can occur in the older individual (Clark, 1977). A decrease in the ability to hear may make participation in social gatherings unenjoyable. Personality and behavior may also be affected by increasing problems with communication and the sense of social inacceptability from their hearing loss (Rockstein & Sussman, 1979). Face to face communication may be necessary for some individuals when giving directions or skill instructions during activities.

When there is a loss in the ability of one or more of the senses, HPRD activities should be planned to augment the remaining senses. In an attempt to optimize the remaining capacities of older adults, emphasis of physical, recreational, and dance activities should shift from speed to accuracy of performance. Shephard (1978) states that, "less important details of tasks are omitted, and there is an increased reliance on previously developed routines of problem solving" (p. 130). A decline in eyesight and learning may also affect an older adult's ability to balance. Activities that stress balance and coordination should be incorporated into physical education, recreation, and dance programs for the older adult. Smith and Gilligan (1983) suggest that the stimulation of muscle proprioceptors during various body movements may help to maintain hand-eye coordination and total body coordination in older adults.

The older adult needs special care and attention, and it is important that the director does not take anything for granted. For example, due to biological reasons, older persons need concrete and clear instructions.

Also, the older adult, as with any adult, needs to feel that he/she can learn at his/her own pace. For this reason, it is important for the director to be patient. When conducting formal games, rules and regulations can be adapted in order to reduce the chance of injury and ensure successful performance. For HPRD programs to serve the elderly effectively, wellness programs and activities must develop programs that are medically and physiologically sound, economically feasible and motivationally attractive. Such programs will possess some of the same objectives as the wellness programs for the younger population, but also address needs unique to the elderly.

General leadership guidelines will be followed by specific ways professionals in health, physical education, recreation and dance can respond to these unique needs of older adults.

General Leadership Guidelines

1. Assess the needs in the community for an organized active recreation and health education program for the elderly. Will this type of program compliment existing programs available for this age group? Communicate with Golden Age Groups, AARP Chapters, Area Agency on Aging Service Centers, church groups, nursing homes, and personal care homes to see if there is an interest in this type of program.

2. Select and train leadership. It is important that the leaders know basic anatomy and physiology of the human body as well as the biomechanical needs of this special population. In addition, they should be familiar with normal changes caused by aging and deconditioning. Retired individuals who have been trained in health education, physical education, recreation and dance would be ideal for the leadership of this type of a program. The leader of the recreation program should have current knowledge of cardiopulmonary resuscitation (CPR) techniques.

3. Discuss the proposed program with local health service personnel. Ask for their assistance in the development of a medical screening form. The physicians will be involved in signing forms, so their input is important.

4. Establish an advisory committee composed of the leaders of various senior citizens groups in the community. They will be valuable when planning times to meet, activities, and best ways to publicize the program. The advisory committee can establish the initial goals of the program. The goals could be modified later by the participants in the program.

5. Develop a program that will meet 2–3 times a week with alternate activities suggested for "off" days. If the program is to end after a given number of weeks, plan a culminating event. If the program

is on-going, plan several "big events" such as a health fair or senior games. Pre-assess the level of knowledge and abilities of the group and plan periodic evaluation sessions to see if the objectives (goals) of the program are being met.

6. Always begin the program on time. Older adults do not follow the same hectic schedule most professional people have and they usually will be in place and waiting for the program to begin at the designated time.

7. The leader should dress appropriately for the setting and the activity. Older people generally do not appreciate short shorts and tight blue jeans. Neat, clean professional looking warm-ups are appropriate in most settings.

8. The leader should become acquainted with the participants as quickly as possible. If the group is large, use name tags so all can be called by name. Some older people prefer to be called by their last name so let them fill out the name tag with preferred name.

9. Communicate with all elderly—well and frail—as adults. Use professional terms, explaining the meaning as the program progresses.

10. Every senior citizen program should have a well-defined emergency plan for the leaders to follow in the event of a cardiac arrest or other accidents.

Health Education Programming

Physical Needs. Well planned health-management programs will enhance the individual physical needs of older adults as well as provide an outlet for psychological stress and tensions. Wellness programs for the older adult should seek to educate this population as to the causes of physical deconditioning and its relationship to the physical needs of the elderly. Physicians and exercise specialists have recommended physical exercise as a preventive and rehabilitative health measure, especially for the sedentary adult.

Health programs should particularly stress the cardiovascular system. The bulk of the research has indicated that regular physical activity and good health practices may reduce the risk of coronary heart disease. As discussed earlier, exercise may improve the circulation of blood through the vascular system and improve metabolism. This may protect the heart from the stress of ischemia and increase cardiac glycogen stores and metabolic capabilities. Physical activity will enhance the mechanical and contractile properties of the heart, maintaining or increasing the heart's ability to pump blood to body tissues. A decrease in blood pressure may occur, thus reducing the amount of work for the heart (McArdle, Katch, & Katch, 1981; Pollack, Wilmore, & Fox, 1978).

24

Good nutritional and exercise habits have been found to normalize the blood-lipid profile and establish a more favorable blood clotting mechanism (McArdle, Katch, & Katch, 1981). Research has also indicated that the level of high-density lipoproteins (HDL) in the bloodstream increases with regular participation in exercise programs. High levels of HDLs have been related to decreased risk of coronary heart disease. Research indicates levels of low-density lipoproteins (LDL) in the bloodstream are not affected by exercise (U.S. Department of Health and Human Services, 1981).

Overweight individuals are prone to elevated lipid levels in the bloodstream, hypertension, and diabetes. Exercise and good health habits may result in weight loss and fat reduction, helping to lower cholesterol and triglyceride levels as well as blood pressure (McArdle, Katch, & Katch, 1981). For diabetes, exercise may decrease the need for insulin (Guyton, 1981).

As mentioned in part two, the basal metabolic rate generally declines in old age and people become less active. To avoid weight gain, the older person must consume no more calories than he or she expends. Health instructors should encourage more activity for all older adults and advise shorter recuperation periods in bed following illness whenever possible. The average caloric intake recommended for people 75 years and older is 2,050 calories per day for men and 1,600 calories per day for women (Whitney & Hamilton, 1981).

Twelve to 20 percent of the calories consumed in the older adult's diet should consist of protein. Fat intake should account for no more than 30 percent of calories consumed and the remainder of the diet should consist of complex carbohydrates (Whitney & Hamilton, 1981). Fat consumption should consist of foods high in unsaturated fat and low in cholesterol to aid in decreasing cholesterol, triglyceride, and LDL levels in the blood (McArdle, Katch, & Katch, 1981; Miller & Allen, 1979).

Salt consumption should also be moderated. Researchers have noted that hypertensive individuals who reduce their salt intake may lower their blood pressure. The estimated safe and adequate intake of sodium is 1.1 to 3.3 grams per day (Whitney & Hamilton, 1981). In order to decrease salt consumption, older adults should lower their intake of high-sodium foods and should not add salt to food in the kitchen or at the table (Roe, 1983).

A broad selection of foods from different food groups will assure a quality diet for an older adult. Carbohydrate, fat, protein, vitamin, and mineral intake may be regulated by consuming foods from the four basic food groups: dairy products; meat and other protein sources; vegetables and fruits; and breads and cereals. It has been indicated that foods from these four groups complement one another in supplying needed nutrients for older adults. A daily diet for elderly people should include two servings

25

of dairy products, one to two servings from the meat and protein group, four servings from the vegetable and fruit group, and four servings from the bread and cereal group.

If the recommended number of servings from the four food groups is not consumed, individuals risk deficiencies of specific nutrients. An overabundance of choline can cause B6 deficiency, which may in turn lead to a reduced amount of iron absorption (Mindell, 1979). A lack of dairy products, for example, may lead to deficiencies in calcium, vitamin D, and riboflavin. A deficiency in vitamin C can also occur from inadequate consumption of vegetables or fruits (Roe, 1983). Moreover, appropriate consumption of fruits, vegetables, and whole grain cereals adds bulk and fiber to the diet of older adults. Fiber is important in maintaining the health of the muscles of the intestinal tract, decreasing the occurrence of constipation. It has also been found that some fibers bind cholesterol and carry it out of the body (Whitney & Hamilton, 1981).

HPRD wellness programs should also improve understanding of the respiratory system and health-management practices that enhance the functional capacity of the lungs. Smoking, stress management, and drug-awareness classes educate the elderly as to proper breathing techniques and chemical agents, including prescription and over-the-counter drugs that affect the respiratory system. Health programs should emphasize that participation in physical, recreational, and dance activities helps decrease stiffening and calcification in the chest cavity and lungs that may occur with advancing age. Conversely, lack of exercise will decrease the intensity of lung contractions needed for breathing, reducing the functional capabilities of the respiratory system (Leviton & Campanelli, 1980).

Health programs should also address the value of flexibility exercises and the types of exercises which enhance range of motion. Static stretching, or a holding position, are most effective because they present the least risk of injury and require less energy. Ballistic stretching, or a bouncing motion, may also be effective if the bouncing motion is very slight. Forceful, rapid bouncing however, activates the muscles' stretch reflex, causing muscular contraction and increasing the chance of injury. It has been recommended that some of the most important flexibility exercises for older adults are ones that involve neck and shoulder flexion, back extension, hip flexion, and ankle flexion (Miller & Allen, 1979).

Many older adults need information on muscle strengthening techniques and exercises. Three types of muscle contractions are known to increase the strength of a muscle: concentric, eccentric, and isometric contractions. Concentric contractions require a muscle to shorten in length while a constant tension is applied. Work with weights and sit-ups involve concentric contractions. Eccentric contractions involve gradual lengthening of a muscle from a shortened position. Slow movement of weights against the pull of gravity induces a muscle to remain at a constant length during a contraction, as occurs when pushing or pulling against a stationary object (Miller & Allen, 1979).

Exercises combining concentric and eccentric contractions are recommended by exercise specialists because they contribute to joint flexibility. The dynamic exercise involved in concentric and eccentric contractions increases muscle strength and endurance while enhancing muscles' aerobic capacity. This type of exercise also helps to improve the stroke volume of the heart (Bruce, 1984; A.C.S.M., 1980).

By contrast, isometric exercises are not recommended for the elderly because they may strain the cardiovascular system. Increased blood pressure during this type of contraction impairs the venous return of blood to the lungs and decreases cardiac output.

Four types of exercise increase both flexibility and strength: passive, assistive, active, and resistive. Passive exercise requires an assistant to move a specific body part of another individual through a range of motion. Assistive exercise involves an individual who helps move a body part through a range of motion to the extent of the individual's need. Exercise in which an individual moves the body part against the force of gravity without assistance is termed active resistance. In resistive exercises, an individual works against some form of resistance (Leviton & Campanelli, 1980).

Health educators have indicated that bone-mineral decline in older adults, called osteoporosis, may be avoided through proper nutrition and regular physical activity (Smith, 1981; Whitney & Hamilton, 1981). Physical activity affects bone in two ways. First, physical activity places increased stress on the skeletal system, creating an increase in cellular activity in the bone and in the amount of bone mineral. Second, physical activity increases the metabolic demands of working muscle, which also increases circulation in the bone, providing valuable nutrients for bone maintenance (Smith, 1981).

Researchers stress that middle-aged individuals and older adults should be educated to prevent the occurrence of osteoporosis by incorporating regular physical activity into their lives. Bone loss may be slowed, prevented, or even reversed by physical exercise (Whitney & Hamilton, 1981).

Low calcium intake in the diet contributes to osteoporosis in older adults, as does reduced absorption or increased excretion of calcium. For men, the minimum daily calcium requirement is above 400 milligrams; women after menopause need 1,000 milligrams a day. It has been recommended that women take in 1 to 1.5 grams of calcium a day, which is equal to approximately five cups of milk. For older women, a reduction of estrogen secretion in the body accelerates bone loss.

Older adults also need information about age related changes in the nervous system. These changes are extremely important because the nervous system coordinates the activities of all other systems of the body. The most common change is related to the cell itself. For example, the cell number decreases with age, while the remaining cells may drastically alter in structural characteristics (Shephard, 1978). McArdle, Katch and Katch (1981) stated, "It's tempting to speculate that the biological aging of certain neuromuscular functions can be somewhat retarded by regular participation in physical activities" (p. 428). It has been found that movement times for simple and complex tasks are significantly faster for active older adults than for older adults who are less active (McArdle, Katch, & Katch, 1981).

Psychological Needs. The older adult needs to be educated on various health topics, such as nutrition, first aid, and stress management. Lectures on health education for the elderly are one means of informing older individuals about these topics. They can be provided by HPRD professionals and also infused within programs and activities.

Nutrition education—an examination of the types and amounts of food required as one ages—may aid indirectly in the prevention of two of the major health problems in the United States: heart disease and stroke. The severity and frequency of these conditions may be alleviated by improving nutritional habits. Overweight, a major contributor to these conditions, may be controlled through sound nutritional practice.

Lectures on nutrition should be developed so that the participants interact and learn from one another. One idea is to have one participant plan a well-balanced menu for another participant based on his or her lifestyle. This technique enables participants to interact with each other and creates a sense of social support within the group.

First aid is another important area to be included in health lectures and should address prevention of household accidents. Older individuals who find it difficult to react quickly must take measures to be prepared in case of an accident. First aid supplies should be in a safe, convenient place. Elderly clients should understand common bodily injuries such as sprains, strains, simple fractures, burns, and lesions. Taping procedures and proper moving techniques should be emphasized.

This type of lecture is an opportunity to build a social network among the participants. In simulated accident situations, for example, participants learn to depend on each other. For example, two participants play the roles of victims in a car accident (makeup and plastic costuming add credibility). The remaining members of the group, who were taken out of the room, then return. They must first assess the situation and then treat the "victims." A special amount of trust must be present in order for the participants to properly adhere to the situation. This type of exercise helps the elderly learn about themselves and stimulates interest in the importance of social support.

Lectures dealing with stress management can help participants identify sources and symptoms of stress in their lives. As discussed earlier, a stress is any development perceived by an individual as potentially harmful, unpleasant, or damaging in relation to the individual's ability to adapt. Common sources of stress in old age are separation, deprivation, loss (death), and unwanted changes such as retirement, a decrease in physical capacity, or a declining income.

Stress is not always negative; indeed, it is essential to life and health. Positive events, such as job promotion, childbirth, and marriage are also considered stressors. Stress keeps one alert, enables one to experience life with depth and to learn from experience. Without a certain amount of stress, a person would not be motivated to carry out even routine tasks. The key to stress management is to balance useful stress and harmful stress.

Some of the common approaches to managing stress are exercise, relaxation meditation, nutrition, and social activities. Through regular exercise, older adults gain confidence in their ability without fear of injury. The latter consideration is extremely important, since the risk of injury increases with age. Relaxation meditation relieves tension and increases one's awareness of the body's reactions to various stimuli. If one can observe and identify reactions to stimuli, one deals with the specific stresses more easily. Finally, associating with others may aid in the elimination of common stress, whether one discusses a specific problem or simply socializes. Nutrition's relation to stress is discussed in another section of this manuscript.

Health Education Guidelines
1. Plan programs with as much participation as possible.
2. Encourage the older adults to suggest topics of interest to them.
3. Programs could be presented by voluntary and nonprofit health agencies in the community. For example:
   Alcoholics Anonymous
   American Health Association
   American Cancer Society
   American Lung Association
   American Red Cross
   Arthritis Foundation
   Asthma and Allergy Foundation
   Health Education Services
   Mental Health Association
   National Council on Alcoholism
   National Health Council
   National Safety Council

29

The following are governmental agencies that provide information in the health field:

    High Blood Pressure Information Centers
    National Clearinghouse on Drug Abuse Information
    National Health Information Clearinghouse
    National Heart, Lung and Blood Institute
    National Institute on Alcohol Abuse and Alcoholism
    National Institute of Mental Health
    U.S. Department of Health, Education, and Welfare
    U.S. Department of Health Promotion and Education
    U.S. Office of Health Information and Health Promotion

4. Select visual aids that minimize the need for visual acuity or precise discrimination. For example, don't use slides or transparencies with small print.
5. Place yourself so that you can be seen and heard easily.
6. Talk slowly and clearly.
7. Determine the medium that facilitates learning for older adults, i.e., auditory, visual, tactile or some combination.
8. Seek feedback from the older adult regarding such things as pace, speech intelligibility, and meaningfulness of the subject content. The instructor may want to utilize evaluation sheets.
9. Select a time for teaching when the person is not preoccupied with other concerns, i.e., recovery from an illness, grief, or finances.
10. Relate new learning to the past and present experience of the older adult.
11. Integrate new behaviors with established and on-going behavior activities so as to enhance memory.
12. Establish goals for learning that are mutually agreed upon by the older adult and the instructor.
13. Establish achievable short-term goals and relate them to long-term goals.
14. Determine what constitutes positive reinforcement for each individual.
15. Provide opportunities for successful learning, prompt feedback, and ample reinforcement for the older adult.
16. Encourage the older adult to help decide when, how, and what they will learn.
17. Utilize terminology and examples familiar to the individual.

Physical Education Programming

Physical Needs. Physical needs that involve movement help keep older adults active and help prevent hypokinesis. As previously discussed, physical fitness for the older adult is defined as the ability to carry out daily activities easily with ample energy left to meet emergency situations and to enjoy leisure activities (P.C.P.F.S., 1973). Smith and Gilligan (1983) stated, "by participating in a total physical activity program, the older adult can improve all aspects of body function. Research has demonstrated improvements of the cardiovascular system, muscles, bone, lungs, and overall work capacity through regular physical activity" (p. 101).

Clark (1977) indicated that a lack of adequate physical activity is related to 80 percent of the incidences of lower back pain in older adults. He noted that active adults tend to age more slowly, have lower blood pressure, are stronger and more flexible, have greater breathing capacity, and maintain proper weight. Clark also reported a link between lack of exercise and emotional difficulties and suggested that physically active adults show greater adaptability to stress, less neuromuscular tension, and more energy.

Before an older adult begins a physical fitness program, medical clearance from a doctor must be obtained (see Appendix B). The doctor's clearance should include medical history, physical examination, and if possible, a laboratory evaluation. A comprehensive medical history consists of information about a person's medical and surgical history, family history, and habits, including cigarette smoking, diet, alcohol consumption, previous physical activity, environment, and daily stresses. A physical examination performed by the physician should emphasize the cardiovascular and respiratory systems, which are heavily affected by exercise. The laboratory evaluation can follow, which may include blood and blood-lipid analyses; as well as an exercise tolerance test.

After appropriate medical clearance has been obtained, a maximal or submaximal exercise tolerance test that stresses the cardiovascular and respiratory systems should be administered (American College of Sports Medicine (A.C.S.M.), 1980. This test should be conducted by a physician and an exercise test technician. The test usually consists of stepping, walking, walk-running, running, or bicycling. Smith and Gilligan (1983) have suggested the Balke treadmill test and the bicycle ergometer test by Pollock et al. as good exercise tolerance tests for the older adult. Smith and Gilligan have also suggested the administration of a sitting-chair step test when use of a treadmill or bicycle ergometer is not possible.

By means of an exercise tolerance test, the individual's maximum heart rate and changes in blood pressure are determined. Also established by the test is the individual's MET (A.C.S.M., 1980). A MET is a multiple of the resting metabolic rate. One MET is equivalent to the resting metabolic oxygen consumption. A MET can also be expressed in terms of oxygen consumption per unit of body weight, with 1 MET equal to approximately 3.6 ml. kg. min.

The MET level is determined by dividing the exercise metabolic rate by the resting metabolic rate. The exercise metabolic rate is the maximum oxygen consumption (VO2) of the individual during exercise and the

31

resting metabolic rate is the maximum oxygen consumption (VO2) of an individual at rest. The MET ratings are utilized to classify the difficulty of sustained physical activity in terms of its strenuousness (McArdle, Katch, & Katch, 1981). Thus, the maximal exercise tolerance test provides the information necessary to establish a specific, individualized exercise prescription for an elderly adult. That prescription should specify physical activities of appropriate type, duration, intensity, and frequency for the individual (A.C.S.M., 1980).

The exercise prescription should also seek to improve the individual's performance in the five basic components of physical fitness: cardiovascular endurance; muscular endurance; muscular strength; flexibility; and body composition (Smith & Gilligan, 1983; A.C.S.M., 1980). Each participant in a fitness program should be pretested to determine which of these areas needs emphasis.

Cardiorespiratory endurance is the functional efficiency of the heart and lungs measured by a maximal exercise tolerance test. Submaximal exercise tests, which estimate the maximal capability of the heart and lungs, are measured in specific performance criteria either related to heart rate or work performance, and have also been devised to measure cardiorespiratory endurance. Individual cardiorespiratory endurance levels are established by comparing maximal and submaximal test results with norms for males and females in specific age categories (Smith & Gilligan, 1983; McArdle, Katch, & Katch, 1981).

Muscular endurance is a measure of ability to persist in a localized muscular effort. Muscular endurance tests measure the ability of an individual to perform a specific activity and low-resistance activity continuously over a specific amount of time. Examples of tests to measure muscular endurance are a two minute sit-up test or repetitive lifting of a specific weight in a specific amount of time (Miller & Allen, 1979). The step test measures muscular endurance of the lower extremities (Smith & Gilligan, 1983).

Muscular strength is a measure of the maximum force or tension generated by a muscle or muscle groups. There are four ways of measuring muscular strength. Tensiometry measures the pulling force of a muscle during a static or isometric contraction. These tests are used for evaluating strength impairment in specific muscles weakened as a result of disease or injury. Dynamometry measures strength on the principle of compression. These devices measure the amount of external static force which can be applied. One repetitive maximum refers to the maximal amount of weight lifted one time during the performance of a standard weight-lifting exercise. The fourth way of measuring muscular strength is through the use of sensitive instruments which measure force, acceleration, and velocity of body segments in various movement patterns. One test for muscular strength in older adults includes use of a hand grip dynamometer, which provides an indication of the strength of the hand and forearm muscles (McArdle, Katch, & Katch, 1981).

Flexibility is the ability of an individual to move the body joints through a maximum range of motion and is related to body size, sex, age, and movement habits. Active individuals tend to be more flexible than inactive individuals because soft tissues and joints shrink when maintained in a shortened position (McArdle, Katch, & Katch, 1981; Miller & Allen, 1979). For the older adult, increased flexibility aids in stooping, bending, and reaching in everyday activities (Smith & Gilligan, 1983). Flexibility tests, designed to measure movement in relation to an absolute performance goal, include the sit n' reach test; the shoulder lift test; and the trunk extension test.

Body composition, the fifth component of physical fitness, is an evaluation of the structural components of the body—muscle, skin, bone, and fat. Indirect techniques such as hydrostatic weighing, skinfold measurements, and circumference measurements are used to assess individuals' fat/lean composition (McArdle, Katch, & Katch, 1981).

Walking, running, bicycling, swimming, and aerobic dance are all physical activities older adults can participate in to improve cardiorespiratory endurance, muscular endurance, and body composition. The maximum heart rate and MET level determined from the exercise tolerance test must be known in order to determine the intensity at which an individual will perform a physical activity.

The maximum heart rate and MET level of an individual are linearly related. Smith and Gilligan (1983) stated, ". . . a subject performing at 50 percent of maximum MET level will reach a heart rate approximately halfway between resting and maximum." For the older adult, the intensity of exercise should be between 40 and 70 percent of the individual's maximum MET level. Exercise at an intensity above 85 percent of the maximum MET level will place excessive stress on the body and might be hazardous to individuals with exercise limitations (Bruce, 1984).

Note that an individual's heart rate is approximately 20 beats per minute lower in physical activities performed in water as compared to activities performed on land. For example, if an individual's 70 percent maximum heart rate is 150 beats per minute, a water activity should be performed at no greater than 130 beats per minute. The average maximum MET level for a young-old adult (55–75 years) ranges from 5 to 7 METs and for the old-old (75 years and over) maximum MET level is 2.5 METs (Smith & Gilligan, 1983).

Before exercise, muscle groups around the major joints of the body should be properly stretched and warmed for at least 10 minutes. Warm-up exercises will help to increase the range of motion of body joints, minimize the possibility of joint or muscle injury, prepare the heart for activity, and help to minimize soreness after exercise. Examples of flexibility exercises which may be utilized as warm-ups are listed at the end of this section (McArdle, Katch, & Katch, 1981; Miller & Allen, 1979).

The total exercise duration for activities like walking, running, bicycling, swimming, and aerobic dance should be at least 20 to 30 minutes. The frequency of the physical activity should be at least three times a week (Bruce, 1984; Smith & Gilligan, 1983; Miller & Allen, 1979). The duration of exercise for the older adult may last longer than for younger adults because the older adult exercises at a lower intensity. Calories burned during exercise should be around 10 percent of an individual's daily caloric intake (Smith & Gilligan, 1983).

It is also important that the elderly understand how to monitor their heart rate before, during, and after exercise. The resting heart rate should be taken before exercise while seated. Then, during exercise, the heart rate should be taken two or three times. Heart rates during exercise show whether an individual is working between 40 and 70 percent of the maximum heart rate. If below 40 percent, exercise intensity should be increased. If greater than 70 percent, exercise intensity should be decreased (Smith & Gilligan, 1983; Miller & Allen, 1979).

Approximately two minutes after completing the prescribed exercise, the individual should take his or her heart rate again, comparing it to the rate before exercise. This last heart rate is called the recovery heart rate (Miller & Allen, 1979).

At the end of the 20 to 30 minute exercise period, cool-down exercises lasting 10 minutes or longer should be performed incorporating the same type of flexibility exercises used during warm-up. Cool-down allows an individual to stretch muscles that may have tightened during exercise, assist in bringing the heart rate back to normal, and helps to minimize muscle soreness.

As previously mentioned, a complete physical fitness program should include activities that will improve muscular strength. An older adult can increase muscular strength by stressing specific muscle groups two or three times a week. For older adults, strengthening programs for the quadriceps, back, abdominal, and arm muscles should be emphasized. A sampling of muscular strength activities appears at the end of this section; these activities also improve muscular endurance (Smith & Gilligan, 1983).

Many fitness programs, such as the increasingly popular outdoor fitness trails, are designed to promote all five components of physical fitness as well as balance and coordination (Smith & Gilligan, 1983). Walking or running on these trails enhances cardiorespiratory endurance, muscular endurance, and body composition. Muscular strength activities include stations along the trail with pulley weights or other lifting equipment. Other stations require the participant to perform flexibility exercises. Walking a balance beam and walking or running through tires strengthen the individual's sense of balance and coordination.

Dance is another excellent physical activity that develops balance, coordination, cardiorespiratory endurance, muscular endurance, flexibility, and body composition. Dance incorporates a wide variety of movements including bending, stretching, twisting, and turning to the beat of music. Serfass (1981) studied the effects of dance-related movement exercise on the flexibility level of elderly subjects with a mean age of 72 years. Elderly subjects who participated three times a week for 12 weeks increased their range of motion in six major points.

Leviton and Campanelli (1980) indicated two goals of teaching dance to elderly subjects—to maintain and enhance functional capacities such as flexibility, endurance, and cardiovascular functioning; and to enhance balance, coordination, kinesthetic awareness, and spatial relationships. Of course, dance may be considered either a physical fitness activity incorporating the five components of fitness or a recreational activity depending upon the intensity of activity (Appendix A). Even recreational dance, however, improves flexibility, muscular endurance, balance, and coordination.

Fitness instructors for older adults should plan individualized programs to meet the needs of each person. Physical fitness activities should be conducted so that participants can see improvements, and have fun.

The following is a list, but not all-inclusive, of exercise/activities for the older adult that may be used to improve the five fitness parameters and enhance the psychological well-being of the older adult:

Cardiorespiratory Endurance (CR)/Muscular Endurance (ME)

Aerobic Dance (CR & ME)
Basketball (CR & ME)
Bicycling (CR & ME)
Circuit Training (CR & ME)
Fitness Trails (CR & ME)
Country Western Dancing (CR & ME)
Cross-country Skiing (CR & ME)
Exercises performed in a chair (CR & ME)
Folk Dance (CR & ME)
Racquetball (CR & ME)
Running (CR & ME)
Swimming (CR & ME)
Tennis (CR & ME)
Therapeutic Dance (CR & ME)
Walking (CR & ME)
Walking/running (CR & ME)
Calisthenic Exercise (ME)
Push-ups (ME)

Sit-ups (ME)
Wall Push-ups (ME)

Flexibility

Static stretching exercises involving all joints of the body should be used. For example:
Lateral neck stretches
Shoulder and pectoral stretches
Back extensor stretches
Upper trunk stretches
Lower trunk stretches
Lateral abdominal stretches
Trunk twisters
Lower back stretches
Hamstring stretches
Lower leg stretches
Foot and ankle stretches

Muscular Strength

The best muscular strength programs involve the use of exercise equipment such as:
Cybex—instrumentation system for testing and evaluation of muscular strength
Free Weights—barbells, dumbbells
Nautilus—instrumentation system for strength development. Resistance throughout the range of motion
Universal Gym—instrumentation system used for strength development
Circuit training and some calisthenic exercises are also effective in building strength in older adults.

Body Composition

The addition of exercise to a program may favorably modify the composition of the body. However, the exercise needs to be aerobic in order to aid in weight loss. For example:
Running
Calisthenic Exercises
Swimming
Walking
Cross-country Skiing

Psychological Needs. Physical education activities can provide psychological benefits to the elderly by helping them to establish and achieve personal goals. Wellness programs should be developed with the intention of meeting the specific needs that will aid in the completion of goals. In addition, HPRD programs, particularly those that require more than one person, encourage a spirit of support and cooperation. In well-designed activities, the elderly develop interpersonal relationships that lead to feelings of acceptance.

Wellness programs may also help the elderly gain insight into their physical capabilities. Often, once a person reaches his or her potential in relation to a new skill, that person will increase in their emotional stability which can lead to increased self-esteem.

Physical education programs should be fun. Designing a program according to the desires of the participants helps to ensure that it will be a source of enjoyment for all.

Exercise Guidelines

Note: The active recreation guidelines should also be followed for a successful exercise program.

1. Be consistent in teaching an exercise program. Begin with a general warm-up which should become routine for the participants. Add new elements to the main activities while maintaining a few familiar ones. The cool-down after exercise should also become routine for the senior citizens. They will enjoy leading the warm-up and cool-down portions of the exercise program.
2. Keep a record of the activities and the intensity level so progression can be built into the program and to show the senior citizens how much they have improved.
3. Tell participants how they will benefit from each activity. This will help them to develop a base of knowledge to plan their own activities when they are not participating with the organized group, e.g., sitting with legs extended and touching toes will stretch the hamstring muscles in the back of the leg which will allow freer movement at the hip joint.
4. Avoid competition in the fitness program. Everyone should progress at his/her own pace.
5. Establish long-term goals in the exercise program that are mutually agreed upon by the older adult and the instructor. Also establish short-term goals that are achievable and related to long-term goals.
6. Do all exercises slowly.
7. Do not hold a position more than 3 to 5 seconds (isometric contraction).
8. Breathe normally when exercising. Avoid holding breath, especially on isometric exercise.
9. Use a hand support on standing exercises.

10. Encourage the use of good, erect posture while performing exercises.
11. Have the senior citizen use the following procedure to get down on the floor safely: Hold onto a chair or table. Bend knees, and go down on knees one at a time. Put hands on floor. Finally, stretch out on the floor. When ready to get up, reverse the process.
12. In all balance activities, keep eyes focused on a non-moving object.
13. For individuals with arthritis, emphasize activities such as swimming and cycling and avoid jogging or running which will cause more pain to arthritic lower extremities.
14. Perform sit-up exercise with legs bent at least 60 degrees. This will lessen the probability of increasing the curvature in the lower back (lordosis) and will require more work on the part of the abdominal muscles.
15. Stretching movements should be done slowly without a jerky or bouncing motion.
16. Avoid deep knee bends. Flexion of the knee to the level of sitting in a chair will provide sufficient exercise to strengthen the quadriceps muscle group on the anterior surface of the thigh.

Recreation/Leisure Programming

Physical Needs. The purpose of recreational and leisure activities for older adults, in terms of physical fitness, is to improve movement. Programs should incorporate muscular endurance activities and flexibility exercises. These activities may also enhance neural functions necessary for movement and increase balance and coordination. In addition, any recreational or leisure activity involving movement will help in keeping older adults active and avoid hypokinesis. Therefore, instructors should plan recreation programs that provide active games and exercises using all parts of the body. Even though recreation and leisure programs do not always stress the cardiovascular and respiratory system to the extent of physical fitness activities, it is suggested by the authors that medical approval from a participant's physician be required before any involvement in the program.

Leviton and Campanelli (1980) made innovative activity suggestions for older adults that may be incorporated into recreational and leisure programs. Each of the following categories includes a variety of activities that may be used by instructors: ball exercises, bar exercises, bean-bag exercises, carrying exercises, chair exercises, companion exercises, club exercises, dramatic exercises, elastic exercises, educational exercises, expression exercises, flag exercises, field exercises, hoop exercises, locomotor exercises, log exercises, marching exercises, mimetic exercises, natural exercises, obstacle exercises, pole exercises, rhythmic exercises, rope exercises, stretching exercises, and wand exercises.

The following is a list of recreational and leisure activities that respond to both the physical and psychosocial needs of the older adult:

      Badminton
      Ballroom dancing
      Bowling
      Canoeing
      Golf
      Hiking
      Horseback riding
      Skiing
      Slow walking
      Softball
      Table tennis
      Therapeutic dance
      Therapeutic recreational activities—(rhythm games with musical instruments, use of objects for manipulation—soft armature wire, elastic tubes, small scarves, streamers, puppets)
      Volleyball

Psychosocial Needs. Recreation has been defined as "selective activities in which gratification of present needs, wants, desires, or objectives takes precedence over practical preparation for later gratification" (Gordon & Guitz, 1976). Both recreation and leisure activities are associated with pleasure and immediate rather than delayed gratification.

Recreation programs should emphasize the emotional benefits of activities, including a feeling of acceptance among peers, enhanced self-image, improved outlook, better sleep, and less psychological need for stimulants or tranquilizers.

By mastering a specific action, the elderly gain a sense of achievement and self-worth. Often, learning a new task will divert attention from personal problems. Success in recreational and leisure activities may also restore confidence and a sense of security. Recreation programs should strive to increase socialization by promoting interpersonal relationships.

Since many older adults experience an increase in the amount of leisure time in their life, it is important to provide a variety of leisure activities. One of the best and most common recreational activities for older adults is work. Through community involvement in projects and organizations, bored or isolated individuals become involved in life, gain social contacts, and build feelings of self-worth. Older adults are a valuable community resource which should not be wasted; their experience and skills are sorely needed by the community.

One way of serving the community is as a volunteer, enabling one person to provide a direct service to another. Volunteer work may range from helping a sick neighbor to working every day in a professional setting, such as a hospital or art center. Indeed, older adults can serve the community in a variety of ways, volunteering as an aide in the public schools, libraries, or programs for handicapped people. Being involved in the community does not always require the older adult to provide a work service. Joining the community theater or church choir is another way to become involved. This type of volunteering will aid in personal satisfaction, since it is personally enjoyable for the participant.

A well designed HPRD wellness program can help place older adults in volunteer positions. Programs can also prepare older adults for work in professional organizations that require trained people.

Travel is another excellent recreational activity for older people. Traveling may range from community tours to long term vacation resorts. Among the most popular form of travel are cultural tours to surrounding areas, plays, movies, and sporting events.

Camping is increasingly popular with older adults. It can help older adults realize their potential for self-sufficiency. Camping gives participants an opportunity to depend on others, along with the responsibility of caring for others. Thorough planning is vital to the success of a camping trip. The instructor must remember that older adults have different needs and desires than younger adults and safety is often the foremost concern. The campsite should be close to a phone or some type of civilized area. First aid kits should be well stocked. The instructor must know participants' physical condition and be prepared to handle any situation that may arise. Ideally, camping trips should be led by more than one person. Preparing the campsite can be strenuous and many older adults may find it difficult to secure tents or prepare a campsite.

Recreational and leisure activities can also include arts and crafts classes and exhibitions. Such activity allows the older adult to experiment with their artistic ability. In addition, arts and crafts programs provide the older adult with the opportunity to socialize and establish relationships gradually.

Games such as chess, shuffleboard, or bingo can offer similar benefits. They also present an opportunity to improve physical skills which in turn may boost self-esteem.

In all recreation and leisure activities, older adults should be allowed to set their own goals; no activity should be performed without a purpose. Older adults, like other people, are highly individual in their choices of goals and purpose. For some individuals, the competition inherent in certain games is purpose enough; competition enables these individuals to explore their mental and physical capabilities. They feel better about themselves by knowing that they control their own destiny.

It should be noted, however, that not everyone enjoys competition. For many, the main goal of recreational activities is to socialize. These individuals need a chance to meet new people and learn a new skill without competition.

Recreation/Leisure Guidelines

1. Plan a program that will allow some level of participation by all individuals for all of the schedule time. Some will be ready for a high level of physical activity, while others will need less stressful activities.
2. For active recreation programs, plan a program of active games and exercises that use all parts of the body before the activity program is completed.
3. Speak clearly and slowly. Avoid yelling; older people have difficulty hearing high pitched sounds. Use "expanded speech" by putting space between words rather than running all of the words in a sentence together.
4. Present the instruction with a slow pace and clear demonstration, allowing the older person time to process the information.
5. Plan activities that do not require fast reaction time and explosive power as these skills become increasingly more difficult for the older person. Response time generally declines with age presenting a safety hazard in some activities.
6. In active recreation programs, watch the individuals in groups closely for signs of stress, such as extremely red or pale face, nausea, heavy breathing, or difficulty in maintaining the pace of the activity. This is particularly important in hot, humid weather. If most individuals in the group are deconditioned, plan activities so that there is recovery time after more strenuous activities.
7. Maintain good eye contact with the participants. Individuals with a hearing loss will be able to watch your lips and follow the directions for the activity.
8. Have fun! If the leader is not enjoying the program, the participants will probably not enjoy it either.

Dance Programming

Physical Needs. The use of dance to respond to older adults' physical needs was addressed in the sections pertaining to physical education and recreation. Many of the activities incorporated in these two areas involved dance, therefore, the physical needs are extremely similar.

Psychosocial Needs. Dance is considered an effective prescription against physical and psychosocial deterioration in the elderly (Leviton & Campanelli, 1980). More specifically, expression of feelings through creative

41

dance can ease problems resulting from isolation, depression, stress, or anxiety.

Dance also promotes group interaction and sociability. It may enhance caring within the group.

To discuss the benefits of dance more fully, it is important to identify the purpose of dance in wellness programs. In this monograph, three types of dance will be addressed: creative movement, therapeutic movement, and the art of dance.

Creative dance incorporates exercise with pleasure by encouraging expression of feelings. It can also improve self-esteem by increasing participants' awareness of their creative capabilities and improving body awareness. In addition, creative dance may be used to increase eye contact, touching, and other forms of nonverbal communication (Leviton & Campanelli, 1980), thus developing mutual support among participants.

Creative dance can play a critical role in addressing the issue of body image, a common concern among the elderly. Body image comprises all of an individual's attitudes about size, weight, strength, shape, proportions, and mobility (Leviton & Campanelli, 1980), thus developing mutual support among participants.

Creative dance aims to provide the elderly with the opportunity to express feelings while improving physical conditioning. This type of dance must always be designed for the individual participant in the wellness program. The instructor must thoroughly assess each individual's physical limitations and needs. For example, two of the most common health problems of the elderly, arthritis and heart disorders, critically affect mobility. But, properly developed, a therapeutic dance program can use exercise and relaxation to facilitate flexibility, circulation, balance, and coordination. Improvement in these areas prevents or relieves many of the physical problems of the elderly.

Wellness leaders must work with clients' physical limitations. A person in a wheelchair or with a walker, cane, or crutch, can work creatively, using various implements for support (Leviton & Campanelli, 1980). Moreover, exercise should be performed without stress or tension; flexibility and relaxation activities can help here. The art of dance, the last area of dance considered here includes ballroom, folk, aerobics, square, and cultural dance. These types of activities increase support since each participant must depend on others to complete the dance successfully. The elderly also improve their perception of themselves by learning a new skill.

HPRD wellness programs for the older adult can achieve remarkable goals if designed properly and implemented correctly. A comprehensive program embraces elements of health, physical education, recreation/leisure, and dance and is developed with the physical and psychosocial needs of the elderly in mind. The program must be presented in an atmosphere that is relaxed and comfortable, contributing to an enjoyable experience for each participant. Many such programs are appearing all over the country. Three exemplary programs are outlined in Appendix C. Each program is specifically designed for elderly participants. Locale and other social factors vary for each of the programs; therefore, there is a noticeable variation in program design. Programs in dance, depending on the activity level, should follow the guidelines described for either the exercise or recreation/leisure guidelines.

References

Adrian, M. J. (1981). Flexibility in the aging adult. In E. L. Smith & R. C. Serfass (Eds.), *Exercise and aging: The scientific basis* (pp. 45–57). Hillside, NJ: Enslow Publishers Inc.

American College of Sports Medicine. (1980). *Guidelines for graded exercise testing and exercise prescriptions* (2nd ed.). Philadelphia, PA: Lea and Febiger.

Botwinick, J. (1973). *Aging and behavior: A comprehensive integration of research findings* (1st ed.). NY: Springer Publishing Co.

Bruce, R. A. (1984). Exercise, functional aerobic capacity, and aging: Another viewpoint. *Medicine and science in sports and exercise, 16,* 8–13.

Carp, F. M. (1968). Some components of disengagement. *Journal of Gerontology, 23,* 282–386.

Clark, H. H. (Ed.). (1977). *Physical fitness research digest.* Washington, DC: President's Council on Physical Fitness and Sports (Series 7, No. 2).

Crandall, R. C. (1980). *Gerontology: A behavioral science approach.* Massachusetts: Addison-Wesley.

Cummings, E., & Henry, W. E. (1961). *Growing old: The process of disengagement.* New York: Basic Books.

Edington, D. W., & Edgerton, V. R. (1976). *The biology of physical activity.* Boston, MA: Houghton Mifflin Co.

Gordon, C., & Guitz, C. (1976). Leisure and lives: Personal expressivity across the life span. In Binstock & E. Shanas (Eds.), *Handbook of aging and the social sciences.* NY: Van Nostrand Reinhold Co.

Guyton, A. C. (1981). *Textbook of medical physiology* (6th ed.). Philadelphia, PA: W. B. Saunders Company.

Harris, C. (1978). *Fact book on aging: Profile of America's older population.* Washington, DC: National Council on Aging, Inc.

Jensen, C. R., & Schultz, G. W. (1977). *Applied kinesiology.* New York, NY: McGraw-Hill Inc.

Lemon, B. W., Bengtson, V. L., & Peterson, J. A. (1972). An exploration of the activity of aging activity types and life satisfaction among inmovers to a retirement community. *Journal of Gerontology, 27,* 511–523.

Leviton, D., & Campanelli, L. (Eds.). (1980). *Health, physical education, recreation, and dance for the older adult: A modular approach.* Reston, VA: American Alliance for Health, Physical Education, Recreation, and Dance. (ERIC Document Reproduction Service No. ED 190 564)

Maddox, G. L. (1963). Disengagement theory: A critical evaluation. *The Gerontologist, 4,* 80–82.

McArdle, W. D., Katch, F. I., & Katch, V. L. (1981). *Exercise physiology.* Philadelphia, PA: Lea & Febiger.

Miller, D. K., & Allen T. E. (1979). *Fitness: A lifetime commitment.* Minneapolis, MN: Burgess Publishing Co.

Mindell, E. (1979). *Vitamin bible.* NY: Warner Books, Inc.

Munns, K. (1981). Effects of exercise on the range of joint motion in elderly subjects. In E. L. Smith & R. D. Serfass (Eds.), *Exercise and aging: The scientific basis* (pp. 167–178). Hillside, NJ: Enslow Publishing Inc.

Pollock, M. L., Wilmore, J. H., & Fox, S. M. (1978). *Health and fitness through physical activity.* New York: John Wiley and Sons, Inc.

President's Council on Physical Fitness and Sports & Administration on Aging. (1973). *The fitness challenge . . . In the later years.* Washington, DC: U. S. Government Printing Office.

Ringler, R. (1982). *Fourth report to council on program.* National Institute on Aging.

Rockstein, M., & Sussman, M. (1979). *Biology of aging.* Belmont, CA: Wadsworth Publishing Co.

Rodgers, D. (1982). *The adult years.* Englewood Cliffs, NJ: Prentice-Hall, Inc.

Roe, D. A. (1983). *Geriatric nutrition.* Englewood Cliffs, NJ: Prentice-Hall, Inc.

Rose, A. M. (1964). A current theoretical issue in social gerontology. *The Gerontologist, 4,* 46–50.

Schaie, W. K., & Geiwitz, J. (1982). *Adult development and aging.* Boston, MA: Little, Brown and Company.

Serfass, R. C. (1981). Exercise for the elderly: What are the benefits and how do we get started? In E. L. Serfass & R. C. Serfass (Eds.), *Exercise in aging: The scientific basis* (pp. 121–129). Hillside, NJ: Enslow Publishers, Inc.

Shephard, R. J. (1981). Cardiovascular limitations in the aged. In E. L. Smith & R. C. Serfass (Eds.), *Exercise and aging: The scientific basis* (pp. 11–17). Hillside, NJ: Enslow Publishing Inc.

Shephard, R.J. (1978). *Physical activity and aging.* Chicago, IL: Year Book Medical Publishers.

Smith, E. L. (1981). Bone changes in the exercising older adult. In E. L. Smith & R. C. Serfass (Eds.), *Exercise in aging: The scientific basis* (pp. 179–186). Hillside, NJ: Enslow Publishers, Inc.

Smith, E. L., & Gilligan, C. (1983). Physical activity prescription for the older adult. *The Physician and Sports Medicine, 11* (8), 91–101.

Staff of the Senate Special Committee on Aging. (1977, April). *Expenditures for the elderly: How much protection does medicare provide.* Washington, DC: U. S. Government Printing Office.

Taeuber, C. (1983). *American transition: On aging society.* Current Population Reports, Special Studies Series.

Teaff, J. D. (1985). *Leisure services with the elderly.* St. Louis, MO: Times Mirror/ Mosby College Publishing Co.

Tortora, G. J. (1977). *Principles of human anatomy.* San Francisco, CA: Canfield Press.

U. S. Bureau of the Census. *America in transition: An aging society* (Current Population Reports, Series P-23, Publication No. 128). Washington, DC: U. S. Government Printing Office.

U. S. Department of Health and Human Services. (1980–1981). *Administration of aging facts about older Americans.*

U. S. Department of Health and Human Services. (1981). *Cardiovascular primer for the workplace* (NIH Publication No. 81-2210).

U. S. Department of Health and Human Services–Public Health Service. *National Center for Health Statistics.* In press.

Whitney, E. N., & Hamilton, E. N. (1981). *Understanding nutrition.* NY: West Publishing Co.

Williams, M. H. (1983). *Nutrition for fitness and sport.* Dubuque, IA: William C. Brown Co.

Appendix A

Guidelines for Exercise Programs for Older Persons (Age 50 and Older) as Developed by the American Alliance for Health, Physical Education, Recreation and Dance

There can be risk in sudden, unregulated and injudicious use of exercise. However, the risk can be minimized through proper preliminary screening and individualized prescribing of exercise programs. It is important for older persons entering an exercise program to have a medical evaluation by a physician knowledgeable about physical exercise and its implications.

For programs involving vigorous exercises (i.e., exercises that exceed the level of intensity encountered in normal daily activities, such as walking and climbing stairs), the medical evaluation should insure that the individual can participate in vigorous exercise without any undue risk to the cardiovascular and other bodily systems. Normally, a test that ascertains an individual's cardiorespiratory adjustment to the stress of exercise is an advisable part of the examination. Minimally, it would ascertain if the cardiovascular system, by such appropriate indicators as heart rate and blood pressure, can adequately adjust to vigorous exercise.

For exercise programs involving low intensity exercise (i.e., exercises that do not exceed the level of intensity encountered in normal daily activities), participants should have their personal physician's approval.

Regardless of whether or not a program of exercise is vigorous or of low intensity, the following guidelines to insure the safety of the participants are offered:

47

1. In that each person's response to the stress of exercise is specific to that individual, it is important that each person's response to exercise be monitored periodically for signs of undue stress (unduly high heart rate, nausea, dyspnea, pallor, pain). Participants should be taught to monitor their own heart rate and to recognize these indicators of stress. Unusual responses should be reported to the exercise leader immediately. Exercise leaders, also, should be vigilant of these warning signs.
2. Every exercise program must have a well-defined emergency plan for exercise leaders to follow in the event of cardiac arrest or other accidents.
3. Exercise programs must have adequate supervision. Exercise leaders should be trained in Cardiopulmonary Resuscitation (CPR) techniques. At the very minimum, CPR trained personnel should be present during every exercise session or in close proximity to the exercise program.

Approved: Alliance Committee on Aging, 4/14/81, Boston, MA; Alliance Board of Governors, 10/4/81, Reston, VA.

Appendix B

Medical Clearance Form

Your patient _____ has applied to participate in the HPRD Wellness Program. The program will require your patient to participate in moderate physical, recreational, and leisure activities. Participation in the program requires your medical clearance. Please complete the following form, indicating any contradictions which may alter or prevent the patient from engaging in specific activities.

Resting Heart Rate _____

Blood Pressure _____

Heart Attack   Within last year _____   1–2 years _____
    2–5 years _____   5 or more years _____

Chest Pain
  At Rest _____
  During Sleep _____
  With Moderate Exercise _____

Heart Surgery _____

Recent Operations (include dates): _____

_____

Muscle Weakness _____

Cramps in Legs _____

Shortness of Breath _____
  At Rest _____
  With Moderate Exercise _____

Respiratory Disorders: _____

Arthritis _____

Joint Stiffness _____

Neck or Back Disorders _____

Any other medical problems: _____

_____

Medications currently used: _____

   Possible side effects: _____

Does the patient smoke cigarettes, cigars, or a pipe? _____

Comments: _____

_____

_____

Physician's Signature   _____

Address   _____

      _____

      Phone _____

      Date _____

Patient's Signature   _____

Address   _____

      _____

      Phone _____

      Date _____

Appendix C

Exemplary Programs

There are various types of programs offered for the elderly dealing with the areas of Health, Physical Education, Recreation, and Dance. Each program possesses individual goals based on the needs of the participants, location of the program, the socio-economic status of participants, and the educational level of the participants.

The three programs illustrated in this monograph were selected as examples based on the goals of the programs. Three goals were identified for the first program. First, to provide the elderly with the opportunity to learn new skills. The second goal was to emphasize physical fitness and well-being. The third goal was to provide the elderly with the opportunity to have fun. The first program is affiliated with the University of Missouri and takes place in a suburb approximately 12 miles from St. Louis. The second and third programs are in rural settings; however, the third program is more of a camp setting.

The first program is directed by Mr. Bruce Clark. The program has been in existence for ten years, which indicates the success of the program. There are ten employees involved in the program. The coordinator is paid as part of his teaching instruction. There are also four older adults teaching square dance and one older adult teaching yoga. There is also one part-time employee and one student part-time employee. During the course of the semester, there are between six and twenty students to aid as part of a requirement for their college course.

The program is affiliated with the University of Missouri; for this reason, the facilities are shared by the college students and the elderly participating in the program. The program utilizes one gymnasium and balcony area which consists of as much space as two normal classrooms. They also have use of two dance studios, one 25 meter swimming pool, and one racketball court. In the spring, the outdoor practice, such as tennis and golf are utilized.

Transportation is not provided for the participants. It was noted that most participants resided within 10 miles of the campus. It was also noted that the majority of participants have a high school education and are from the low moderate socio-economic status.

When describing the activities involved in the program, it is important to mention that the participants do have input in the types of activities which are offered. In order to determine the interest of the elderly, the program committee has developed an advisory board consisting of six people involved in the program. They meet at least once a semester to discuss the needs, concerns, and attitudes of the participants, as well as accepting any suggestions for new activities. A list of some of the activities utilized in the program is as follows:

Health	Physical Education	Dance	Recreation/Leisure
Health & Fitness Lectures	Aquatics Yoga/Relaxation Lifetime Sports Clinic (1 hr. health lecture, 20 min. warm-up) Choose activity: basketball, volleyball, swimming, golf, tennis, walk/jog	Square: 20–30 people Tap: 45 people Social: 20–30 people Aerobic: # varies	Same as Physical Education

Before entering the program, each participant must have a physician's approval. The participant must also sign a release form.

Mr. Clark commented on suggestions for an institution starting a Health, Physical Education, Recreation, and Dance program for the older adult. He feels the program must be enjoyable and provide the elderly with the opportunity to socialize. Also, he feels the elderly must have input into activity selection.

The second program is located in a rural setting in Western Pennsylvania. The age range of the people participating in the program is from 60 to 96 years of age.

The goals of the program are to develop and implement a complete system of social services for the 60 + population. The program has been in existence for eight years and employees are paid staff. There are five volunteers as well as the aid of the Mercer County Area Agency on Aging, Inc.

The program takes place in a staff center which has a large recreational/dining room, stage, classroom, kitchen, and an office.

Transportation is provided for the participants, since it is a rural setting and not within walking distance for most participants. The educational level of the participants range from the eighth grade through the college level. Most of the participants are reported to be of the middle socio-economic status.

When describing the activities involved in the program, as with the first program, it is important to mention that the participants are encouraged to make suggestions and comments. A list of some of the activities utilized in the program is provided below.

Health
Health Screenings:
Blood Pressure–Monthly
Hearing–Yearly
Visual/Glaucoma–Yearly
Glucose–Yearly

Informative Programs: Monthly
Greenville Hospital
United Community Hospital
Pharmacists

Nutrition Programs: Monthly

Recreation/Leisure
—Bus Trips (day trips up to 10 days)
—Cards
—Puzzles
—Music

Physical Education
—Bowling League 1/wk.
—Exercise Class 3/wk.
—Over 50 Fitness 1/wk.
—YMCA

Dance
Not encouraged because of
church policy where we meet.

—Table Games
—Art Classes
—Life Skill Education Classes in
a variety of areas

Prior to entering the program, each participant must have a physician complete a medical clearance form.

The program is designed to accommodate all areas of Health, Physical Education, Recreation, and Dance. The following is an illustration of a typical exercise session. Music is provided throughout the entire class. The participants are guided through a warm-up, beginning in a chair, walking, and flexibility and strength. They then assume a standing position and engage in aerobic exercise including jogging in place, knee lifts, and leg kicks. After the aerobic portion, the class proceeds through a cool-down.

The following is a list of suggestions for an institution starting a Health, Physical Education, Recreation and Dance program for the older adult.

1. Use medical clearance form.
2. File card with general information, e.g., who to contact in case of emergency and phone numbers.
3. Offer wide variety of programs to include everyone. Individualize.
   Ex. a. chair
       b. floor
       c. standing—with or without chair

    d. aerobic—dance, use of bikes, treadmills, etc.

    e. walking program

4. Monitor HR and BP before and after.

5. Choose music they will enjoy.

6. Offer a variety of exercises to keep classes interesting.

The third program is also located in a rural setting in a location known as Camp Kon-O-Kwee. The age of the participants is 55 years of age and older. The goals of the program are to provide the older adult with the opportunity to gain companionship and strengthen existing relationships with the young as well as old. Also, they will develop new skills and interests in activities that can be pursued after the camping experience. One other goal for the older adult is to participate in new outdoor experiences that would not be available in any other environment. This particular program has been in existence for seven years and employees are paid staff. It was noted that there is always at least one nurse on duty for the residence programs.

The facilities which are utilized include a pool, dining hall, lodge, and recreation fields. Transportation is not provided for the participants since it is a camp setting. The following is a list of activities offered for the older adult.

Health
Drug Interaction
Nutrition Workshop

Recreation/Leisure
Crafts
Nature Hikes
Skits
Bingo

Physical Education
Swimming
Canoeing/Boating
Aerobics
Volleyball
Exercise Class

Dance
Square
Ballroom

These activities are selected upon the results of a written evaluation by participants. Prior to entering the program, the participants are required to have a physical examination by a physician, who must then sign a medical clearance form.

The staff at Camp Kon-O-Kwee recommend that any new program needs to educate the older adult on the benefits of wellness and to cite examples of how a program can help to increase the life span and also improve the quality of life.

Appendix D

Bibliography

Adams, G. M., & deVries, H. A. (1973). Physiological effects of an exercise training regimen upon women aged 52 to 72. *Gerontologist, 28,* 50–55.

Aloia, J. (1981). Exercise and skeletal health. *Journal of the American Geriatric Society, 29,* 104–107.

American College of Sports Medicine. (1978). The recommended quantity and quality of exercise for developing and maintaining fitness in healthy adults. *Medicine and Science in Sports, 10,* vii–x.

American population growing older (p. C11). (1981). New Jersey: Asbury Park Press.

Astrand, P. O. (1968). Physical performance as a function of age. *Journal of the American Medical Association, 205,* 105–109.

Astrand, I., Astrand, P. O., Hallback, I., & Kilbom, A. (1973). Reduction in maximal oxygen uptake with age. *Applied Physiology, 35,* 649–654.

Atchley, R. C. (1971). Retirement and leisure participation: Continuity or crisis? *Gerontologist, 11,* 13–17.

Atchley, R. C. (1977). *The social forces in later life.* Belmont, CA: Wadsworth Publishing Co., Inc.

Atchley, R. C. (1980). *The social forces in later life: An introduction to social gerontology* (3rd ed.). Belmont, CA: Wadsworth Publishing Co.

Atchley, R. C., & Seitzer, M. M. (1976). *The sociology of aging: Selected readings.* Belmont, CA: Wadsworth Publishing Co., Inc.

Barry, A. J., Steinmetz, J. R., Page, H. F., & Rodahl, K. (1966). The effects of physical conditioning on older individuals: II. Motor performance and cognitive function. *Journal of Gerontology, 21,* 192–199.

Bassey, E. J. (1978). Age, inactivity and some physiological responses to exercise. *Gerontology, 24,* 66–77.

Beach, M. (1981, March/April). Business and the graying of America. In *Perspective on aging* (pp. 16–19). National Council on Aging.

Benestad, A. M. (1965). Trainability of old men. *Acta Medica Scandinavia, 178,* 321–327.

Bennett, J., Carmack, M. A., & Gardner, V. J. (1982). The effect of a program of physical exercise on depression in older adults. *Physical Educator, 39,* 21–24. (ERIC No. EJ 260 708)

55

Binkley, A. (1980, January). Assessment of education needs of personnel who provide services to Indiana aged. Doctoral dissertation, Indiana University.

Birren, J. E., & Renner, V. J. (1980). Concepts and issues of mental health and aging. In J. E. Birren & R. B. Sloane (Eds.), *Handbook of mental health and aging* (pp. 4–33). Englewood Cliffs, NJ: Prentice-Hall, Inc.

Birren, J. E., & Renner, V. J. (1977). Research on the psychology of aging: Principles and experimentation. In J. E. Birren & K. W. Schaie (Eds.), *Handbook of the psychology of aging.* New York: Van Nostrand Reinhard.

Birren, J. E., Woods, A. M., & Williams, M. V. Behavioral slowing with age: Causes, organization and consequences. In L. W. Poon (Ed.), *Aging in the 1980's.* Washington, DC: American Psychological Association.

Blumenthal, J., & Williams, R. (1982). *Exercise and aging: The use of physical exercise in health enhancement, 6*(3), 1–5. (Center Reports on Advances in Research, Duke University Center for the Study of Aging and Human Development).

Boarman, A. M. (1978). The effect of fold dancing upon reaction time and movement time of senior citizens. (Doctoral dissertation). *Dissertation Abstract International, 38,* 5329-A.

Botwinick, J. (1978). *Aging and behavior* (2nd ed.). New York: Springer.

Brody, H. (1970). Structural changes in the aging nervous system. In H. T. Blumenthal (Ed.), *The regulatory role of the nervous system in aging.* New York: S. Karger.

Brown, R. S., Ramirez, D. E., & Taub, J. M. (1978). The prescription of exercise for depression. *The Physician and Sportsmedicine, 6*(12), 35–45.

Burke, W. E., Tuttle, W. W., Thompson, C. W., Janney, C. O., & Weber, R. J. (1953). The relation of grip strength and grip-strength endurance to age. *Journal of Applied Physiology, 5,* 628–630.

Butler, R. N., & Lewis, M. I. (1982). *Aging and mental health: Positive, psychosocial and biomedical approaches* (3rd ed.). St. Louis, MO: The C. V. Mosby Co.

Chapman, E. A., deVries, H. A., & Swezey, R. (1972). Joint stiffness effects of exercise on young and old men. *Journal of Gerontology, 27,* 218–221.

Clarke, H. H. (1978). Exercise and aging. In G. Burdman & R. Brewer (Eds.), *Health aspects of aging* (pp. 127–142). Portland, OR: A Continuing Education Book.

Clarke, H. H. (Ed.). (1977). Exercise and aging. *Physical Fitness Research Digest, 7*(2), 1–27.

Colavita, F. B. (1978). *Sensory changes in the elderly.* Springfield, IL: Charles C. Thomas.

Conrad, C. C. (1977). Viewpoint: Regular exercise program is beneficial psychologically as well as physically. *Geriatrics, 29,* 40–44.

Corbin, D. (1981). An exercise program for the elderly. *Physical Educator, 38,* 46–49.

Corso, J. F. (1971). Sensory processes and age effects in normal adults. *Journal of Gerontology, 26,* 90–105.

Crandall, R. C. (1980). *Gerontology: A behavioral approach.* Reading, MA: Addison-Wesley Publishing Co.

Cuellar, J. B. (1980). *Minority elderly Americans: A prototype for area agencies on aging.* San Diego, CA: Allied Home Health Association.

Cureton, T. K. (1969). *The physiological effects of exercise programs on adults.* Springfield, IL: Charles C. Thomas.

deVries, H. (1971). Exercise intensity threshold for improvement of cardiovascular-respiratory function in older men. *Geriatrics, 26*, 94–101.

deVries, H. A. (1976). Fitness after fifty. *Journal of Physical Education and Recreation, 47*, 47–49.

deVries, H. A. (1979). Physiological effects of an exercise training regime upon men aged 52–88. *Journal of Gerontology, 24.*

deVries, H. A. (1975). Physiology of exercise and aging. In D. Woodruff & J. Birren (Eds.), *Aging: Scientific perspectives and social issues.* New York: D. Van Nostrand Co.

deVries, H. A. (1977). Physiology of physical conditioning for the elderly. In R. Harris & L. J. Frankel (Eds.), *Guide to fitness after 50.* New York: Plenum Press.

deVries, H. A. (1974). *Vigor regained.* Englewood Cliffs, NJ: Prentice-Hall.

deVries, H. A., & Adams, G. M. (1972). Comparison of exercise responses in old and young men: I. The cardiac effort and total body effort relationship. *Journal of Gerontology, 27*, 334–348.

Drinkwater, B. L., Horvath, S. M., & Wells, C. L. (1975). Aerobic power of females, ages 10 to 68. *Journal of Gerontology, 30*, 385–394.

Ellfeldt, L., & Lowman, C. L. (1973). *Exercises for the mature adult.* Springfield, IL: Charles C. Thomas.

Falk, G., Falk, V., & Tomashevich, G. V. (1981). *Aging in America and other cultures.* Saratoga, CA: Century Twenty One.

Fitts, R. H. (1981). Aging and skeletal muscle. In E. L. Smith & R. C. Serfass (Eds.), *Exercise and aging.* Hillside, NJ: Enslow.

Frankel, L., & Richard, B. (1977). *Be alive as long as you live: Mobility exercises for the older person.* Charleston, WV: Perventicare Publications.

Franklin, B. A. (1978). Motivating and educating adults to exercise. *Journal of Physical Education and Recreation, 49*, 13–17.

Freakany, G. A., & Leslie, D. K. (1975). Effects on an exercise program on selected flexibility measurements of senior citizens. *Gerontologist, 15*, 182–183.

Garnet, E. D. (1982). *Movement is life: An holistic approach to exercise for older adults.* Princeton, NJ: Princeton Book Co.

George, L. K. (1978). The impact of personality and social status factors upon levels of activity and psychological well-being. *Journal of Gerontology, 33*(6), 840–847.

Gunter, J., & Bratton, R. D. (1980). Senior citizens and bowling: A study in motivation. *Review of Sport and Leisure, 5*, 70–80.

Gutmann, E., & Hanzlikova, V. (1977). Age changes in the neuromuscular system. *Scientechnica*, 80–88.

Harman, D. (1971). Free radical theory of aging: Effect of the amount and degree of unsaturation of dietary fat on mortality rate. *Journal of Gerontology, 26*(4), 451–457.

Harris, R., & Frankel, L. (Eds.). (1977). *Guide to physical fitness after fifty.* New York: Plenum Publishing Corp.

Hartford, M. E. (1980). The use of group methods for work with the aged. In J. E. Birren & R. B. Sloane (Eds.), *Handbook of mental health and the aging* (pp. 806–826). Englewood Cliffs, NJ: Prentice-Hall, Inc.

Hattlestad, N. W. (1979). Improving the physical fitness of senior adults: A state-wide approach. *Journal of Physical Education and Recreation, 50,* 29–31. (ERIC No. EJ 215 184)

Hodgson, J. L., & Buskirk, E. R. (1977). Physical fitness and age, with emphasis on cardiovascular function in the elderly. *Journal of the American Geriatric Society, 25,* 385–392.

Hooks, B., & Hooks, E., Jr. (1981). Needed: Physical educators on the nursing home team. *Physical Educator, 38,* 32–34. (ERIC No. EJ 244 886)

Jable, J. T., & Cheesman, M. J. (1978). An exercise project by young adults for senior citizens. *Journal of Physical Education and Recreation, 49,* 26–27. (ERIC No. EJ 176 547)

Labouvie, E. W. (1980). Identity versus equivalence of psychological measures and constructs. In L. W. Poon (Ed.), *Aging in the 1980's.* Washington, DC: American Psychological Association.

Larson, R. (1978). Thirty years of research on the subjective well-being of older Americans. *Journal of Gerontology, 33*(1), 109–129.

LaRue, A., Jarvick, L., & Hetland, M. (1979). Health in old age: How do physicians' ratings and self-ratings compare? *Journal of Gerontology, 34*(5), 687–691.

Lersten, K. C. (1974). *Some psychological aspects of aging: Implications for teaching and learning.* Paper presented at the Fifth Annual Conference of the Rocky Mountain Education Research Association, Albuquerque, New Mexico. (ERIC No. EJ 109 093)

Leslie, D. K., & McClure, J. W. (1975). *Exercises for the elderly.* Des Moines, IA: Iowa Commission on Aging.

Levin, J., & Levin, W. C. (1980). *Ageism: Prejudice and discrimination against the elderly.* Belmont, CA: Wadsworth Publishing Co., Inc.

Leviton, D. (1974). Toward a humanistic dimension of HPER. *Journal of Physical Education and Recreation, 45,* 41–43. (ERIC No. EJ 092 049)

Lundegren, H. M. (1980). Motivation for participation in adult fitness programs. In G. A. Stull (Ed.), *Encyclopedia of physical education, fitness and sports: Training, environment, nutrition, and fitness.* Salt Lake City, UT: Brighton.

MacNeil, R. (1981). Nursing homes as closed environments: Implications for therapeutic recreation service. In G. Hitzhusen & J. Elliot (Eds.), *Expanding horizons in therapeutic recreation VIII.* Columbia, MO: University of Missouri-Columbia.

McLure, J., & Leslie, D. (1972). Guidelines for an exercise program leader for senior citizens. *Journal of Health, Physical Education, and Recreation, 43,* 72–73.

Mobily, K. (1982). Physical activity and aging. In M. Teague, R. MacNeil, & G. Hitzhusen (Eds.), *Perspective on leisure and aging in a changing society.* Columbia, MO: The University of Missouri.

Montoye, H. J., & Lamphiear, D. E. (1977). Grip and arm strength in males and females, age 10 to 69. *Research Quarterly, 48,* 109–120.

Moritani, T. (1981). Training adaptations in the muscles of older men. In E. L. Smith & R. C. Serfass (Eds.), *Exercise and aging.* Hillside, NJ: Enslow.

Morse, C. E., & Smith, E. L. (1981). Physical activity programming for the aged. In E. L. Smith & R. C. Serfass (Eds.), *Exercise and aging: The scientific basis.* Hillside, NJ: Enslow.

Muiesan, G., Sorbini, C. A., Solinas, E., & Grasse, V. (1971). Respiratory function in the aged. *Bulletin of Physiologicial-Pathological Respiration, 7,* 973–1009.

Murrell, F. H. (1970). The effect of extensive practice on age differences in reaction time. *Journal of Gerontology, 25,* 268–274.

National Association for Human Development. (1976). *Join the active people over 60: A model exercise and fitness program for older persons.* Washington, DC: President's Council on Physical Fitness and Sports.

Nicholas, A. (1977). Community program for tension control. In R. Harris & L. J. Frankel (Eds.), *Guide to fitness after 50.* New York: Plenum Press.

Noble, C. E. (1978). Age, race and sex in the learning and performance of psycho-motor skills. In R. T. Osborne, C. E. Noble, & H. Weyl (Eds.), *Human variation, The biopsychology of age, race and sex.* New York: Academic Press.

Norris, A., & Shock, N. (1974). Exercise in the adult years. In W. Johnson & E. Buskirk (Eds.), *Science and medicine of exercise and sport.* New York: Harper and Row.

Norris, A. H., Shock, N. W., & Yiesngst, J. (1973). Age changes in heart rate and blood pressure responses to graded and standardized exercise. *Circulation, 8,* 521–526.

Osness, W. (1980, April). *Physiological aging and exercise.* Paper presented at the American Alliance for Health, Physical Education, and Recreation annual convention, Detroit, Michigan. (ERIC No. EJ 190 571)

Ostrow, A. C. (1983). Age role stereotyping implications for physical activity participation. In G. Rowles & R. Ohta (Eds.), *Aging and milieu: Environmental perspectives on growing old.* New York: Academic Press.

Ostrow, A. C. (1980). Physical activity as it relates to the health of the aged. In N. Datan & N. Lohmann (Eds.), *Transitions of aging.* New York: Academic Press.

Ostrow, A. C. (1979). *Validation of a conceptual model characterizing attitudes of the elderly toward lifetime sports: A preliminary report.* Paper presented at the Midwest American Alliance for Health, Physical Education and Recreation convention, Madison, Wisconsin.

Ostrow, A. C., Jones, D. C., & Spiker, D. D. (1981). Age role expectations and sex expectations for selected sport activities. *Research Quarterly for Exercise and Sport, 52,* 216–227.

Palmore, E. B. (1979). Predictors of successful aging. *The Gerontologist, 19,* 427–431. (ERIC No. EJ 210 540)

Palmore, E. B., Cleveland, W. P., Nowlin, J. B., Ramm, D., & Siegler, I. C. (1979). Stress and adaptation in later life. *Journal of Gerontology, 34*(6), 841–851.

Palmore, E. B., & Kivett, V. (1977). Changes in life satisfaction: A longitudinal study of persons aged 46–70. *Journal of Gerontology, 32*(3), 311–316.

Parks, C. J. (1979). *The effects of a physical fitness program on body composition, flexibility, heart rate, blood pressure and anxiety levels of senior citizens.* Unpublished doctoral dissertation, University of Alabama.

Plowman, S. A., Drunkwater, B. L., & Horvath, S. M. (1979). Age and aerobic power in women: A longitudinal study. *Journal of Gerontology, 34,* 512–520.

Poon, L. (Ed.). (1980). *Aging in the 1980's.* Washington, DC: American Psychological Association.

Pullias, E. V. (1977). Problems of aging: Psychological principles. *Journal of Physical Education and Recreation, 48,* 33–35.

Renner, J., & Birren, J. E. (1980). Stress: Physiological and psychological mechanisms: In J. E. Birren & R. B. Sloane (Eds.). *Handbook of mental health and the aging.* Englewood Cliffs, NJ: Prentice-Hall, Inc.

Role of exercise in aging. (1979, March). *Update.* Washington, DC: American Alliance for Health, Physical Education, Recreation and Dance.

Shephard, R. J., & Sidney, K. H. (1979). Exercise and aging. In R. Hutton (Ed.), *Exercise and sport science reviews* (Vol. 6). Philadelphia, PA: Franklin Institute Press.

Shephard, R. J., & Sidney, K. H. (1979). Exercise and aging. In R. Hutton (Ed.), *Exercise and sport science reviews* (Vol. 7). Philadelphia, PA: Franklin Institute Press.

Sherwood, D. E., & Selder, D. J. (1979). Cardiorespiratory health, reaction time and aging. *Medicine and Science in Sports, 11,* 186–189.

Shirers, J., & Fait, H. (1980). *Recreational service for the aging.* Philadelphia, PA: Lea & Febiger.

Sidney, K. H. (1981). Cardiovascular benefits of physical activity in the exercising aged. In E. L. Smith & R. C. Serfass (Eds.), *Exercising and aging.* Hillside, NJ: Enslow.

Sidney, K. H., & Shephard, R. J. (1976). Attitudes toward health and physical activity in the elderly: Effects of a physical training program. *Medicine and Science in Sports, 8,* 246–252.

Sidney, K. H., & Shephard, R. J. (1977). Perception of exertion in the elderly, effects of aging, mode of exercise, and physical training. *Perceptual and Motor Skills, 44,* 999–1010.

Smith, B. H., & Sethi, P. K. (1975). Aging and the nervous system. *Geriatrics, 30,* 109–115.

Snyder, E. E. (1980). *A reflection on commitment and patterns of disengagement from recreational physical activity.* Paper presented to the North American Society for the Sociology of Sport convention, Denver, Colorado.

Spirduso, W. W. (1980). Physical fitness, aging, and psychomotor speed: A review. *Journal of Gerontology, 35,* 850–865.

Spirduso, W. W., & Clifford, P. (1978). Replication of age and physical activity effects on reaction time and movement time. *Journal of Gerontology, 33*, 26–30.

Townsend, P. (1981, March). The structured dependency of the elderly: A creation of social policy in the twentieth century. In *Aging and society* (Vol. 1, Part 1).

Tzankoff, S. P., Robinson, S., Pyke, E., & Brown, C. (1972). Physiological adjustments to work in older men as affected by physical training. *Journal of Applied Physiology, 33*, 346–350.

U.S. Department of Health and Human Services. (1981, August). *Special report on aging* (NIH Publication No. 80-2135).

U.S. Department of Health, Education and Welfare. (1975). *The fitness challenge: In the later years* (DHEW Publication No. OHD 75-20802). Washington, DC: U.S. Government Printing Office.

U.S. Department of Health, Education and Welfare. (1979). *Older Americans act of 1965, as amended.* Washington, DC: Government Printing Office.

Walsh, D. A., & Thompson, L. W. (1978). Age differences in visual sensory memory. *Journal of Gerontology, 33*, 383–387.

Wash, P. (1979). *Employment issues in recreation for the elderly.* Washington, DC: Unpublished Bureau of Labs Statistics' Report.

Whithouse, F. A. (1977). Motivation for fitness. In R. Harris & L. J. Frankel (Eds.), *Guide to fitness after 50.* New York: Plenum Press.

Wiegand, R. L., & Ramella, R. (1981). *An examination of psychomotor skill acquisition in relation to information storage and processing capacity among older adults.* Paper presented at the North American Society for the Psychology of Sport and Physical Activity convention, Monterey, California.

About The Authors

Christel M. Smith is Director of the Hamot Wellness Center in Erie, Pennsylvania. She is directly responsible for the planning, organization and implementation of adult wellness and physical fitness programs. Ms. Smith holds a Master of Science degree in Physical Education from Slippery Rock University.

Leslie A. Stenger is Program Director for Bio-Energetiks, a cardiac rehabilitation and health maintenance organization. Her major duties include developing and conducting exercise sessions, based on exercise tolerance tests results for cardiac patients. Ms. Stenger received her Master of Science degree in Physical Education from Slippery Rock University.